A Planning and

M000121829

THE GREAT CIRCLE CRUISE

AROUND THE EASTERN USA

Author & Publisher...........................G. Bickley Remmey, Jr.

Printer...The Times Publishing Co.
Duquesne, PA 15110

Copyright.......................© 1999 by G. Bickley Remmey, Jr.

ISBN No. 0-9669987-0-7

This book is available by mail from
Bick Remmey, 14 Alton Road, Yardley, PA 19067
or call 215-493-4973.

DEDICATION

This book is dedicated to the first mate Jeri Remmey without whom this trip would not have been possible. The book is also dedicated to all the other crew members who shared our adventure.

Buzz Mead
Bob Lande
Charlotte Lande
Anne Gardner
Bill Gardner
Nancy Hoffman
Jim Hoffman
Kathryn Doherty
Len Doherty
Charlie Frame
Anaruth Hynson
George Hynson
Bonnie Remmey
Scott Remmey
Maria Doelp
Peter Doelp
Helen Roth
George Roth
Kathy Remmey
Bick Remmey, III
Betty Ann McArdle
Jim McArdle
Claudine Remmey
Chris Remmey

ABOUT THE AUTHOR

Bick Remmey got a late start in cruising, beginning in 1989 at the age of 54 with the purchase of *"Fanta-Sea"*, a 27 foot Carver Express Cruiser. Based out of Avalon, New Jersey, over the next four years, Bick and Jeri Remmey cruised to Washington D.C., to North Carolina, plus four trips to the Chesapeake. In 1994, they purchased *"Nittany Navy"*, a 36 foot Carver Aft Cabin Motor Yacht, which was ideal for two couples with staterooms at opposite ends of the boat, each with their own head. In 1994 and 1995, they made another two Chesapeake trips plus a 1,250 mile round trip to Montreal, Canada, all with a crew of four.

Along with their cruising experience, Bick and Jeri both took the U.S. Power Squadron Public Boating and Seamanship Courses. Bick also took the piloting and advanced piloting courses, and in 1993, he got his Captain's License from The Coast Guard.

In June 1996, the Remmeys started the *"Great Circle Cruise"* and completed it in July 1997.

CONTENTS

CONTENTS

PHOTO CONTENTS

PHOTO CONTENTS

PHOTO CONTENTS

Choices

If the idea of taking the longest one-way inland cruise possible in the United States (approximately 5400 miles) appeals to you, then read on. A cruise that includes the Atlantic intracoastal waterway, the Erie Canal, the Great Lakes, the Mississippi River, the gulf intracoastal waterway and the Florida Keys. This cruise allows you to see the United States in a very different way from travelling on land or in the air. The cruise is an adventure, a learning experience and lots of fun.

Most people who make this trip are retired or take a year off from work. However, we took the trip and I'm not retired and I didn't take a year off. The time to do the trip varies between 18 weeks (I don't think you would want to do it any faster) to one year with the difference being the speed of your vessel and the amount of time you choose to stay at each port. Most of the people whom we met doing the great circle cruise were from Florida and were doing the trip in six months. Typically, they left Florida on the first of May and returned home at the end of October. People who take a year to do the trip usually spend the entire winter in Florida and/or the Bahamas.

I am a consultant who is under contract with a flexible work schedule. We did the trip in 18 weeks spread over 57 weeks, with half the trip in 1996 and the other half in 1997. Our first leg was Avalon, New Jersey to Chicago in 6 weeks (June 7 to July 16). The second leg was Chicago to New Orleans in 4 weeks (September 9 to October 7). The third leg was New Orleans to West Palm Beach in 5 weeks (January 17 to February 22, 1997), and the last leg was West Palm Beach to Avalon, New Jersey in 3 weeks (June 15 to July 11, 1997). In other words, in 1996, we cruised for 10 weeks and had 42 weeks for work; while in 1997, we cruised for 8 weeks which left 44 weeks to work.

It isn't necessary to wait until you are retired or until your children grow up to make the trip. One couple that I heard about took their children out of school (2nd grade and 7th grade) for a year, and their mother, who was a school teacher, tutored them in their respective grades with an approved correspondence course for the year of their cruise. Therefore, "When to Make the Trip" is the first major decision to be made. I first started thinking about making the trip in 1991, and I assumed that we would make the trip in the year 2000 after retiring at age 65. At the time, we had a 27 ft. Carver Express cruiser that we kept at our shore house in Avalon, New Jersey and took once a year to the Chesapeake for a two week cruise. It was fun to dream about the big cruise around the Eastern United States.

Once I got serious about the trip, I realized I would need to know more about boating and navigation. I was already a member of the U.S. Power Squadron, so I signed up for their navigation courses, piloting and advanced piloting which were very helpful. In January 1993, I passed the Coast Guard exam for my captain's license. It is not necessary to have a captain's license to make this trip, but it is very helpful, especially with regards to the rules of the road on our waterways.

A lot of factors go into that first major decision "when to make the trip". If you are already retired and already have the right kind of boat you are ready to go any time. However, if you are not retired, you must decide how much time to take off (18 weeks to a year) and when you can do that. I guess for most people, the easiest time to take the trip would be their first year of retirement. However, for those who have an interest in taking their children out of school and offering them an adventure like this, you probably will never regret the decision.

The time between when you decide you want to take the trip and when the trip starts can be lots of fun. For us, this period was 5 years - 1991 to 1996. We spent three years going to boat shows to find the right boat for the trip. After we decided on the exact boat we wanted for the trip, we had to find one for sale since we decided to buy a used boat to save money. In June of 1994, we found the boat and bought it. Since our whole family had graduated from Penn State (my wife and I plus our three sons), we named the boat "Nittany Navy". In July 1995, we took the "Nittany Navy" on a 1,250 mile, three-week inland cruise from Avalon, New Jersey (near Cape May, N.J.) to Montreal, Canada and back. Besides having a wonderful vacation, this trip prepared us for the big trip in a number of ways. We learned about locks (60 of them). We learned that we needed a back up G.P.S. for the Loran, and that we needed 100 feet of hose, etc. The fall of 1995 and spring of 1996 were spent getting charts, waterway guides, planning our detailed itinerary and getting all of our guest crew members organized.

Once you have decided when you are going to take the trip, the next important decision is how many people will be on board, usually one, two, three or four. This decision can also determine what size boat you take.

Obviously, if you are doing the trip single handed, the boat could be quite small. Most people make the trip with two on board. However, we did most of the trip with a crew of four. Our crews mostly consisted of my wife and I, plus another couple who shared a week or 10 days with us. In total, we had thirteen different crews.

One can make the trip in a sailboat, but it is not the ideal type of boat for this trip. During most of the inland portion of the trip, the mast would have to be taken down and put into a horizontal trestle to permit the sailboat to get under hundreds of low bridges. The maximum boat height above the water line for this trip is 19 feet and 15.5 feet the way we went. This means that a sailboat would have to make most of the trip under power. Also, the draft of a sailboat is a problem. A trawler is probably the most economical type boat for this trip, however, the mast will probably have to be hinged to get under the 19 ft. limit. A sport fisherman or convertible can be used so long as the height stays under 19 feet. Most express cruisers will not have a height problem even though they can be quite large (50 feet long). We chose an aft cabin motor yacht because it maximized the living space and was ideal for two couples with a stateroom and head at opposite ends of the boat. Our boat was 16 feet 3 inches high to the top of the radome with an overall length of 42 feet, a 14 ft. beam and a 37" draft.

Another important consideration is gas versus diesel. Since gas engines are much cheaper to buy and diesel engines are cheaper to run, the best choice depends on a number of factors. If your normal boating use is less than 100 hours per year, not counting this trip, you probably are better off with gas. If your normal boating use is over 100 hours per year, diesel could be justified. This trip is approximately 360 hours run time when cruising at 18 knots and averaging 15 mph including slow areas. The same trip is 720 hours when cruising at 7.5 knots. Our average seasonal usage cruising around the Chesapeake was 80 hours so we chose gas.

Once you have decided on the size of the boat, the style of the boat, and the type of power, you are ready to start shopping.

The next decision is new or used. New boats have the advantage that you order them just the way you want them and they have new engines. Used boats cost a lot less. We bought a four-year-old boat that looked like new but had 500 hours on the engines and did not have an aft deck enclosure which we wanted. We added the aft deck enclosure to make the boat just the way we would have ordered it and the savings over the new boat were still substantial.

The economics of this trip can vary substantially. A 40 ft. single engine diesel trawler cruising at 7 knots could do the entire trip with as little as 2,000 gallons of fuel. Whereas, we used about 9,000 gallons of gas cruising at 18 knots most of the time. If we had cruised at 10 mph like we did in the Erie Canal, we would have used only 5,000 gallons for the whole trip. If we had kept our 27 ft. boat, we would have also used much less fuel. In other words, the amount of fuel you use not only depends on the size of your boat but how fast you run it. If you are going to take a year to do the trip, it makes sense to cruise at slower speeds to save fuel.

The next major cost is staying in marinas versus anchoring out. The average cost in a marina was $1.00 per foot per night. Our boat is 36 feet at the water line, so we paid an average of $36.00 per night. If you anchor out, your only cost is the fuel to run the generator ($2 to $10) for air conditioning, lights, etc.

Another major cost variable is eating in restaurants or cooking on board. We ate breakfast and lunch on board and almost always ate dinner in a restaurant. However, if you cook on board, it obviously cost a lot less. The economics are such that if you compare a 40 ft trawler with a single diesel engine cruising at 7 knots, that anchors out and cooks on board to a 40 ft. gas powered motor yacht cruising at 20 knots, staying in marinas and eating out, the total cost for two people could vary from $50 to $250 per day or more. Therefore, the cost of the trip depends on the choices you make.

In summation, the list of choices you will make are as follows:

1. When to take the trip.
2. How long the trip is (18 weeks to a year).
3. How many people on board.
4. What size boat.
5. What type boat.
6. Gas or diesel.
7. New or used boat.
8. Cruising speed.
9. Stay in marinas or anchor out.
10. Eat in restaurants or cook on board.

The Route

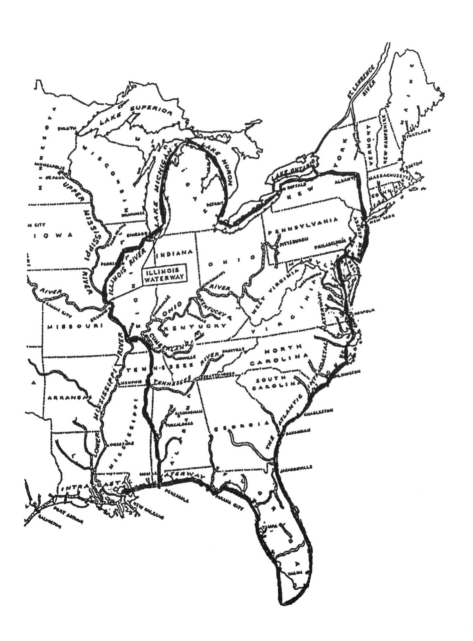

Where you start and end the cruise depends on where you live.

The route passes through or borders 20 states plus Ontario, Canada. People from New England can join the cruise at New York. People from the upper Midwest can join the cruise at St. Louis from the upper Mississippi River or the Missouri River.

The cruise passes through the following major cities:

New York	**St. Louis**	**Jacksonville**
Buffalo	**Mobile**	**Savannah**
Cleveland	**New Orleans**	**Charleston**
Detroit	**Tampa**	**Norfolk**
Chicago	**Miami**	**Baltimore**

And could easily include:

Toronto
Milwaukee
Philadelphia
Washington DC

As previously stated where you start and end the cruise depends on where you live. The route map on the previous page shows the entire route. The most popular direction to go is counter clockwise because most of the river currents, including the Mississippi River, are flowing that way. Also, the prevailing winds on the gulf are West to East. It is obviously possible to go clockwise, however, a trawler that cruises at 7 knots would have difficulty bucking a 5 to 6 knot current in the Mississippi. This book assumes that the route is counter clockwise.

The timing of the trip depends on where you start. The Erie Canal is closed from early November to late April depending on the weather. In 1996, the Canal did not open until early June because of high water levels from spring rains. Since half the trip is in fresh water, ice is a problem in the winter and early spring. Therefore, the Erie Canal and the Great Lakes should only be done in the summer. Assuming you stick with the two rules of "counter clockwise" and "Erie Canal and Great Lakes only in the summer", the timing for your trip will be determined by your starting point. The following are some examples:

STARTING POINT	BEGIN TRIP
New York	June
Chicago	September
New Orleans	February
Miami	April

One of the great things about this trip is that it is a leisurely sight seeing tour of the Eastern United States, which is the reason that it is almost entirely on inland waterways. The only times when the cruise is not on an inland waterway are as follows:

1. Cape May, New Jersey to New York Harbor -- run 2 miles off shore in Atlantic Ocean for 150 miles.

2. Carrabelle, Florida to Tarpon Springs, Florida -- 180 miles across the gulf, can be done in two days. First day Carrabelle to Cedar Key, Florida (120 miles) and second day Cedar Key to Tarpon Springs (60 miles).

3. Marco Island to Key West -- 98 miles across the gulf.

4.   Key West to Marathon -- run outside in the Ocean for 43 miles re-enter intracoastal waterway at Marathon.

Note: Passages 3 and 4 above are eliminated if you take the Okeechobee waterway from the West coast of Florida to the East Coast.

There is a variation in the route that depends on the height of your boat. If your boat is 15 feet 6 inches or less you can stay on the Erie Canal all the way to Buffalo. However, if your height above the water line is between 15 feet 6 inches and 19 feet (maximum height for this trip), you must take the Erie Canal to Oswego, New York on Lake Ontario. From Oswego you cruise west on Lake Ontario to the Welland Canal which connects into Lake Erie near Buffalo. Allow a full day to go through the Welland Canal System because the large commercial boats (1,000 feet long) travelling on the Saint Lawrence Seaway have the right-of-way and it is not uncommon for pleasure boats to wait hours at each lock.

You will note that the route only spends 230 miles on the Mississippi and then goes 60 miles up the Ohio River to the Tennessee River. This route is called the Tenn-Tom and is a parallel route to the Mississippi to get to the gulf. The Tenn-Tom route was opened in 1985 when a canal system was completed that connected the Tennessee River with the Tombigbee River to provide an alternate route to the Mississippi. The lower Mississippi is mainly a barge river and is relatively unfriendly for pleasure boats. There are long distances (200 miles) between gas stops and marinas are few and far between. The barge traffic is very heavy and the swift current often carries large debris such as telephone poles. By comparison the Tenn-Tom is tranquil, there is very little current, much less barge traffic, and gas stops and marinas are less than 100 miles apart. The Tenn-Tom is also very scenic.

As you can see on the route map, the Tenn-Tom brings you into the gulf at Mobile AL which means that you have to backtrack 160 miles to get to New Orleans. On the other hand, the Mississippi goes right to New Orleans. In other words, staying on the Mississippi would be faster especially with a slow boat because of the swift current. A boat with a range of 300 miles or more would not have a fuel problem, however, you would have to anchor out sometimes, and it can be hard to find moorings out of the current with sufficient depth. The main reason most people prefer the Tenn-Tom to the lower Mississippi is that it avoids the swift current and the large floating debris problem.

There is another option in the route and that is the Okeechobee waterway that goes from Fort Myers on the West Cost of Florida to Stuart on the East Coast. By taking this route you must backtrack to visit South Florida and the keys.

A summary of the choices you have in the route are as follows:

1.   Lake Ontario and the Welland Canal versus the western half of the Erie Canal.

2.   The lower Mississippi River versus the Tenn-Tom Waterway.

3.   The Okeechobee waterway versus sailing directly to Key West from Naples.

Planning

We spent many many hours over a two-year period planning this trip. Therefore, one of the main purposes of this book is to simplify the planning for others. The steps involved in planning the trip are as follows:

1.   Buy all the waterway guide books listed below.

Waterway Guide   Price
To order call 800-233-3359

- ***Waterway Guide - Northern***
  C & D Canal to Erie Canal $33.95

- ***Waterway Guide - Southern***
  New Orleans to Jacksonville, Florida $33.95

- ***Waterway Guide - Mid-Atlantic***
  Jacksonville, Florida to C & D Canal $33.95

Lakeland Boating
To order call 800-892-9342

- ***Ports O'Call Lake Erie & St. Clair***
  Buffalo to Port Huron $44.95

- ***Ports O'Call Lake Huron***
  Port Huron to Mackinac Island $44.95

- ***Ports O'Call Lake Michigan***
  Mackinac Island to Chicago $44.95

Quimby's
To order call 314-241-7354

- ***Cruising Guide***
  Chicago to Mobile, AL $17.45

2. Determine the time frame for the trip. This includes the overall length of the trip as well as the starting date. You will recall in Chapter 2 we discussed the fact that the starting date depends on where you live.

3. Determine the average number of miles per day that you would like to cover when cruising. This will depend on the speed of your boat and the number of hours you wish to run. We averaged 15 miles per hour and I like to run about 5 hours so that I used 75 miles per day for planning. (To average 15 miles per hour we cruised at 17 knots.) Actually our run times varied from as little as 1 hour to a maximum of 10 hours on several occasions.

4. Using the waterway guides, select the ports close to your daily range. Once you have selected the ports using the waterway guides, you can select the marina and or anchorage where you would like to stay. The waterway guides list detailed information on each marina in a port area. To select a marina, I first checked to see if they offered transient slips. Next, I checked to see if they had gas, then 50 amp electricity, and lastly if they had a restaurant. For two day layovers, I also looked to see if they had laundry facilities. If you choose to anchor out instead of renting a slip, the waterway guides are excellent sources for anchorage locations.

All the marinas where we stayed are listed in Chapters 5 through 17 with lists of services. I would stay at these same marinas again. The marinas listed are not necessarily the ones originally selected. What happened was as we traveled and talked to people we met, they recommended marinas in areas they were familiar with, and if they were different than the marinas I had selected, I changed to the one recommended.

5.   Write an itinerary which lists the dates, ports and distances. In writing the itinerary which is your master cruising plan, I would suggest a one-day layover every four or five days to do laundry. I would also suggest one day per week be allowed for bad weather assuming you would stay in port. This means that, exclusive of sight seeing days, you would plan to cruise no more than 5 days per week. Using our situation as an example, we could have done the 5,400 mile trip at 75 miles per day in 72 days total. We actually did the trip in 125 days, which I think is a minimum. If I were retired, I would have taken more time, such as 180 days.

The actual itineraries that we used are as follows. Since we did the trip in four legs I wrote an itinerary for each leg.

LEG 1
1623 MILES - 40 DAYS
AVALON, NJ to CHICAGO, IL

DAY			STATUTE MILES
1. Friday June 7, 1996		Avalon, NJ to Manasquan Inlet, NJ Brielle Yacht Club (908) 528-6250	96 miles

2.   Saturday   Manasquan Inlet to   63 miles
     June 8, 1996   Tappan Zee Bridge
                      Tarrytown Marina, NY
                      (914) 631-1300

3.   Sunday   Tappan Zee Bridge to   109 miles
     June 9, 1996   Troy, NY
                      Troy Town Dock Marina
                      (518) 272-5341

Erie Canal Info. (518) 471-5011

4.   Monday   Troy to Fultonville, NY   48 miles
     June 10, 1996   Poplars Inn and Marina   12 locks
                      (518) 853-4511

5.   Tuesday   Fultonville to Rome, NY   66 miles
     June 11, 1996   Riverside Marina   8 locks
                      (315) 337-5720

6.   Wednesday   Rome to   58 miles
     June 12, 1996   Baldwinsville, NY   4 locks
                      Coopers Marina
                      (315) 635-7371

7.   Thursday   Baldwinsville to   74 miles
     June 13, 1996   Fairport, NY   7 locks
                      Town Dock

8.   Friday   Fairport, NY to   74 miles
     June 14, 1996   Lockport, NY   2 locks
                      Goehle Municipal Marina
                      (716) 433-9795

9.   Saturday   Lockport, NY to   34 miles
     June 15, 1996   Buffalo, NY   3 locks
                      Erie Basin Marina
                      (716) 842-4141

10.	Sunday June 16, 1996	Buffalo Gardners and Jeri arrive Bob, Charlotte, Buzz leave	
11.	Monday June 17, 1996	Buffalo Drive to Niagara Falls	
12.	Tuesday June 18, 1996	Buffalo to Erie, PA Erie Yacht Club (814) 453-4931 Office (814) 456-9914 Gas Dock	82 miles
13.	Wednesday June 19, 1996	Erie to Cleveland, OH Old River Yacht Club (216) 281-6792	101 miles
14.	Thursday June 20, 1996	Cleveland	
15.	Friday June 21, 1996	Cleveland	
16.	Saturday June 22, 1996	Cleveland to Sandusky, OH Cedar Point Marina (419) 627-2334	64 miles
17.	Sunday June 23, 1996	Sandusky to Put-In-Bay, OH Boardwalk Marina (419) 285-6183	21 miles
18.	Monday June 24, 1996	Put-In-Bay to Detroit, MI Kean's Detroit Yacht Harbor (313) 822-4500	52 miles

19. Tuesday June 25, 1996	Detroit (Enterprise Rent a Car brings car to Marina)	
20. Wednesday June 26, 1996	Detroit Gardeners Fly Home	
21. Thursday June 27, 1996	Hoffmans arrive	
22. Friday June 28, 1996	Detroit to Port Huron, MI Municipal Marina (810) 984-9745	50 miles
23. Saturday June 29, 1996	Port Huron to Harbor Beach, MI Harbor Beach Marina (517) 479-9707	55 miles
24. Sunday June 30, 1996	Harbor Beach to Harrisville, MI Harrisville City Dock (517) 724-5242	55 miles
25. Monday July 1, 1996	Harrisville to Cheboygan, MI Walstrom Marina (616) 627-7105	91 miles
26. Tuesday July 2, 1996	Cheboygan to Mackinac Island, MI Mackinac Island Marina (906) 847-3561	14 miles
27. Wednesday July 3, 1996	Mackinac Island	

28. Thursday   Mackinac Island
     July 4, 1996

29. Friday   Mackinac Island to   50 miles
     July 5, 1996   Petoskey, MI
                       Petoskey Municipal
                       Marina
                       (616) 347-6691

30. Saturday   Petoskey to   15 miles
     July 6, 1996   Charlevoix, MI
                       Dohertys arrive
                       Hoffmans leave
                       Northwest Marina
                       (616) 547-5552

31. Sunday   Charlevoix, MI
     July 7, 1996

32. Monday   Charlevoix, MI
     July 8, 1996

33. Tuesday   Charlevoix to   67 miles
     July 9, 1996   Frankfort, MI
                       Jacobson Marina
                       (616) 352-9131

34. Wednesday   Frankfort to   114 miles
     July 10, 1996   Holland, MI
                       Eldean Shipyard
                       (616) 335-5843

35. Thursday   Holland to   41 miles
     July 11, 1996   Benton Harbor, MI
                       Riverview 1000 Marina
                       (616) 927-4471

36. Friday July 12, 1996	Benton Harbor to Chicago, IL Burnham Park Municipal Harbor (312) 747-7009	53 miles
37. Saturday July 13, 1996	Chicago, IL	
38. Sunday July 14, 1996	Dohertys Leave Chicago to Wilmington, IL Illinois River- mile 273.7 Harborside Marina (815) 476-2254	55 miles 3 locks
39. Monday July 15, 1996	Wilmington, IL to Seneca, IL Springbrook Marina- mile 252 (815) 357-8666	21 miles 1 lock
40. Tuesday July 16, 1996	Dry Dock Boat Limo to O'Hare Fly Home From Chicago	

LEG II
1396 MILES - 29 DAYS
CHICAGO to NEW ORLEANS

DAY   STATUTE MILES

1. Monday September 9, 1996	Fly to Chicago with Charlie Frame Limo to Spring Brook Marina - Seneca, IL (815) 357-8678	

2. Tuesday   Seneca to Henry, IL   IL. R. Mile
September 10, 1996   Seneca, IL   252   56 miles
                      Lock   244.6   2 locks
                      Lock   231.0
                      Henry, IL   196.1
                      Henry Harbor Marina
                      (309) 364-2181

3. Wednesday   Henry to Browning, IL   IL. R. Mile
September 11, 1996   Henry, IL   196.1   99 miles
                      Lock   157.1   1 lock
                      Browning, IL 97.5
                      Rivers Edge Boat Club
                      (217) 323-4780

4. Thursday   Browning to   IL. R. Mile
September 12, 1996   Portage de Sioux, MO
                      Browning, IL 97.5   104 miles
                      Lock   80.2   1 lock
                                     Miss. R.
                      Portage de
                      Sioux, MO   212.4
                      My River Home Harbor
                      (314) 899-0903

5. Friday   Portage to Sioux, MO to
September 13, 1996   Ste. Genevieve, MO   Miss. R. Mile
                      Portage de
                      Sioux, MO   212.4
                      Lock   200.8   90 miles
                      Lock   185.0   2 locks
                      Ste.   122.5
                      Genevieve, MO
                      Marina de Gabouri
                      (573) 883-5599
                      (Get 10 - 5 gal. gas cans
                      to carry extra 50 gal.)

6. Saturday   Ste. Genevieve, MO to
    September 14, 1996 Cairo, IL   Miss. R Mile
                        Ste.   122.5   121 miles
                        Genevieve, MO
                        Anchor out   1.0
                        near Cairo
                        (Add extra 50 gal.
                        to gas tanks)

7. Sunday   Cairo, IL anchorage
    September 15, 1996 to Grand River, KY   Miss. R. Mile
                        Anchorage   1.0   83 miles
                                      Ohio R.
                                      Mile   3 locks
                        Cairo, IL   981
                        Lock   962.6
                        Lock   938.9
                        Tenn. R.   934.2
                        Gas (get rid
                        of gas cans) 928.4
                        Tennessee R   934.2
                        Lock   Tenn. R. Mile
                        (Ky. Dam)   21.0
                        Grand
                        Rivers, KY   on Cumberland R.
                        Green Turtle 1 mile from Tenn. R.
                        Marina
                        (502) 362-8364

8. Monday   Grand Rivers, KY
    September 16, 1996

9. Tuesday   Grand Rivers to   Tenn. R. Mile
    September 17, 1996 Waverly, TN   23.0   92 miles
                        Cuba   115.5
                        Landing Marina
                        (615) 296-2822

10. Wednesday   Tenn. R. Mile
    September 18, 1996 Waverly to
                      Iuka, MS   115.5   104 miles
                      Lock   206.7
                      Tenn-Tom   215.0
                                   Tenn-Tom Mile
                      Tenn-Tom   452
                      Mile
                      Iuka, MS   448.7
                      Acqua Yacht
                      Harbor
                      (601) 423-2222

11. Thursday   Iuka, MS
    September 19, 1996 Charlie Frame Leaves

12. Friday   Iuka, MS
    September 20, 1996

13. Saturday   Iuka, MS
    September 21, 1996

14. Sunday   Iuka, MS
    September 22, 1996 Hynsons and Jeri Arrive
                      from Memphis

15. Monday   Iuka, MS to
    September 23, 1996 Smithville, MS
                                   Tenn-Tom Mile
                      Aqua Yacht
                      Harbor   448.7   72 miles
                      Lock Bay
                      Springs   411.9   4 locks
                      Lock E   406.7
                      Lock D   398.4
                      Lock C   391.0
                      Smithville   376.5

Smithville Marina
(205) 373-6701

16. Tuesday September 24, 1996	Smithville to Carrolton, AL		Tenn-Tom Mile 69 miles
	Smithville Marina	376.5	4 locks
	Lock B	376.3	
	Lock A	371.1	
	Lock Aberdean	357.2	
	Lock Columbus	334.2	
	Carrolton AL	307.4	
	Marina Cove (205) 373-6701		

17. Wednesday September 25, 1996	Carrolton, AL to Demopolis, AL		Tenn-Tom Mile 91 miles
	Marina Cove	307.4	2 locks
	Lock Tom Bevill	306.8	
	Lock Gainesville	266	
	Demopolis, AL	216.7	
	Demopolis Yacht Basin (334) 289-4647		

18. Thursday September 26, 1996	Demopolis to Lady's Landing, AL		Tenn-Tom Mile
	Demopolis Marina	216.7	137 miles
	Lock Demopolis	213.4	2 locks
	Bobby's Fish Camp (gas)	118.9	

```
                          Lock
                          Coffeeville    116.6
                          Jackson, AL
                          Lady's
                          Landing        80.0
                          (205) 246-2903
```

19. Friday   Jackson to   Tenn-Tom Mile
    September 27, 1996   Mobile, AL
                           Lady's
                           Landing   80.0   87 miles
                           Mobile City   0.0
                           Grand Mariner
                           Marina   7.0
                           (334) 443-6300

20. Saturday   Mobile, AL
    September 28, 1996

21. Sunday   Mobile, AL
    September 29, 1996   Hynsons leave

22. Monday   Mobile, AL
    September 30, 1996   Scott and Bonnie arrive

23. Tuesday   Mobile, AL to
    October 1, 1996   Biloxi, MS   85 miles
                           Point Cadet Marina
                           (601) 436-9312

24. Wednesday   Biloxi, MS to
    October 2, 1996   New Orleans, LA   106 miles
                           Orleans Marina
                           (504) 288-2351

25. Thursday   New Orleans
    October 3, 1996

26. Friday   New Orleans
     October 4, 1996

27. Saturday   New Orleans
     October 5, 1996

28. Sunday   New Orleans
     October 6, 1996

29. Monday   Leave boat in the water
     October 7, 1996   fly home to Philadelphia
                               with Bonnie and Scott

LEG III
NEW ORLEANS TO WEST PALM BEACH
1033 S. MILES - 37 DAYS

DAY   **STATUTE MILES**

1. Friday   Fly to New
    January 17, 1997   Orleans, LA
                               Leave Philadelphia
                               8:30 a.m.
                               Arrive New Orleans
                               10:40 a.m.
                               Pick up boat at
                               Orleans Marina

2. Saturday   New Orleans to   106 miles
    January 18, 1997   Biloxi, MS
                               Point Cadet Marina
                               (601) 436-9312

3. Sunday   Biloxi to   97 miles
    January 19, 1997   Pensacola, FL
                               Harbor Village at
                               Pitt Slip
                               (904) 432-9620

4.	Monday January 20, 1997	Pensacola to Destin, FL Sandestin's Baytowne Marina (904) 267-7777	30 miles
5.	Tuesday January 21, 1997	Destin, FL Woodluff's Condo (904) 837-9561	
6.	Wednesday January 22, 1997	Destin, FL Doelps Arrive	
7.	Thursday January 23, 1997	Destin to Panama City, FL Bay Point Marina (904) 235-6911	45 miles
8.	Friday January 24, 1997	Panama City to Carrabelle, FL The Moorings (904) 697-2800	80 miles
9.	Saturday January 25, 1997	Carrabelle, FL	
10.	Sunday January 26, 1997	Carrabelle, FL Doelps Leave Roths Arrive	
11.	Monday January 27, 1997	Carrabelle to Cedar Key, FL Cedar Key Municipal Dock (352) 543-5132	120 miles

12. Tuesday   Cedar Key to   60 miles
    January 28, 1997   Tarpon Springs, FL
                       Port Tarpon Marina
                       (813) 937-2200

13. Wednesday   Tarpon Springs to   65 miles
    January 29, 1997   Longboat Key, FL
                       Longboat Key Moorings
                       (941) 383-8383

14. Thursday   Longboat Key to   43 miles
    January 30, 1997   Boca Grande, FL
                       Millers Marina
                       (941) 964-2283

15. Friday   Boca Grande
    January 31, 1997

16. Saturday   Boca Grande
    February 1, 1997

17. Sunday   Boca Grande
    February 2, 1997

18. Monday   Boca Grande
    February 3, 1997   Roths Leave
                       Bick & Kathy Arrive

19. Tuesday   Boca Grande to   65 miles
    February 4, 1997   Marco Island, FL
                       Marco River Marina
                       (941) 472-5111

20. Wednesday   Marco Island to   98 miles
    February 5, 1997   Key West, FL
                       The Galleon Marina
                       (305) 292-1292

CHAPTER 3

ICW Mile 1243

21. Thursday
    February 6, 1997

    Key West

22. Friday
    February 7, 1997

    Key West

23. Saturday
    February 8, 1997

    Key West
    Bick and Kathy leave

24. Sunday
    February 9, 1997

    Key West

25. Monday
    February 10, 1997

    Key West
    McArdles Arrive

26. Tuesday
    February 11, 1997

    Key West

27. Wednesday
    February 12, 1997

    Key West to
    Marathon, FL
    Faro Blanco Bayside
    (305) 743-9018
    ICW Mile 1193

    50 miles

28. Thursday
    February 13, 1997

    Marathon to
    Key Largo, FL
    Gilbert's Holiday Is.
    at Key Largo
    (305) 451-1133
    ICW Mile 1134

    59 miles

29. Friday
    February 14, 1997

    Key Largo to
    Fort Lauderdale, FL
    Bahia Mar Marina
    (954) 764-2233

    50 miles

ICW Mile 1064

30.	Saturday February 15, 1997	Ft. Lauderdale to Delray Beach, FL Delray Beach Yacht Club (407) 272-2700 **ICW Mile 1039**	25 miles
31.	Sunday February 16, 1997	Delray Beach McArdles Leave	
32.	Monday February 17, 1997	Delray Beach	
33.	Tuesday February 18, 1997	Delray Beach	
34.	Wednesday February 19, 1997	Delray Beach	
35.	Thursday February 20, 1997	Delray Beach	
36.	Friday February 21, 1997	Delray Beach to West Palm Beach, FL Rybovich Spencer Marina SM 1020 (407) 844-1800 **ICW Mile 1029** Leave boat for 4 months	20 miles
37.	Saturday February 22, 1997	Drive to Miami Airport Fly to San Juan Leave Miami 8:50 a.m. Arrive San Juan 12:21 p.m.	

CHAPTER 3

LEG IV
PALM BEACH TO AVALON
1377 S. MILES - 23 DAYS

DAY			STATUTE MILES
1.	Thursday June 19, 1997	Fly to West Palm Beach, FL Leave Philadelphia 10:00 a.m. Arrive W. Palm Beach 12:30 p.m. Get boat at Rybovich Marina	
2.	Friday June 20, 1997	West Palm to Vero Beach, FL Complete Yacht Services (561) 231-2111 **ICW Mile 952**	68 miles
3.	Saturday June 21, 1997	Vero Beach to Titusville, FL Titusville Municipal Marina (407) 269-7255 **ICW Mile 878**	74 miles
4.	Sunday June 22, 1997	Titusville to St. Augustine, FL St. Augustine Municipal Marina (904) 825-1026 **ICW Mile 778**	100 miles
5.	Monday June 23, 1997	St. Augustine Tour St. Augustine	

6.	Tuesday June 24, 1997	St. Augustine to Jekyll Island Jekyll Harbor Marina (912) 635-3137 **ICW Mile 684**	94 miles
7.	Wednesday June 25, 1997	Jekyll Is. to Savannah, GA Savannah Bend Marina (912) 897-3625 **ICW Mile 582**	102 miles
8.	Thursday June 26, 1997	Savannah, GA	
9.	Friday June 27, 1997	Savannah to Charleston, SC City Marina (803) 723-5098 **ICW Mile 469**	113 miles
10.	Saturday June 28, 1997	Charleston, SC Tour Charleston	
11.	Sunday June 29, 1997	Charleston, SC	
12.	Monday June 30, 1997	Charleston to Georgetown, SC Heritage Plantation Marina (803) 237-3650 **ICW Mile 395**	74 miles
13.	Tuesday July 1, 1997	Georgetown to Southport, NC Blue Water	75 miles

Point Marina
1-910-278-1230
ICW Mile 320

| 14. | Wednesday
July 2, 1997 | Southport to
Morehead City, NC
Morehead City
Yacht Basin
(919) 726-6862
ICW Mile 204 | 116 miles |

| 15. | Thursday
July 3, 1997 | Morehead City | |

| 16. | Friday
July 4, 1997 | Morehead City to
Belhaven, NC
River Forest Marina
(919) 943-2151
ICW Mile 136 | 68 miles |

| 17. | Saturday
July 5, 1997 | Belhaven to
Coinjock, NC
Midway Marina
(919) 453-3625
ICW Mile 49 | 87 miles |

| 18. | Sunday
July 6, 1997 | Coinjock to
Norfolk, VA
Waterside Marina
(757) 625-2000
ICW Mile 0 | 49 miles |

| 19. | Monday
July 7, 1997 | Norfolk to
Irvington, VA
Tides Inn
(804) 438-5000 | 70 miles |

20. Tuesday   Tides Inn to   70 miles
    July 8, 1997   Solomans, MD
                   Harbor Island Marina
                   (410) 326-3444

21. Wednesday   Solomans to   80 miles
    July 9, 1997   Baltimore, MD
                   Baltimore Inner
                   Harbor Marina
                   (410) 837-5339
                   (Chris and Claudine arrive)

22. Thursday   Baltimore
    July 10, 1997

23. Friday   Baltimore to   137 miles
    July 11, 1997 Avalon, NJ

END OF TRIP

Outfitting The Boat

This chapter covers the special things you will need on your boat for the "*Great Circle Cruise*". This chapter does not list all the standard things that every boat should have such as life preservers, flares, a compass, etc.

1.   Charts

I chose to have charts for every step of the way because I always like to know exactly where I am in a boat. It is possible to do the rivers and canal systems without charts, but there are times when two rivers come together and the chart tells you which is the right way to go. The charts are also needed if you plan to do much anchoring out.

I purchased the charts for the trip in December 1995 at which time electronic charts were not as detailed and were much more expensive than standard charts. I realize that electronic charts are getting better and cheaper, however, the charts listed here are all standard charts.

Individual NOAA charts purchased separately are usually more expensive. Therefore, the most economic way of buying charts is in the form of chart books, if available. Boat/US offers discounted prices on chart books covering the Great Lakes and the coastal areas.

Charts available from Boat/US
To order call (800) 937-2628 (Prices shown are from their 1997 catalog.)

- *Richardson's Chart Book & Cruising Guide - Lake Erie Edition*
  Item 694401-10 $64.95

- Chart #74 S. Lake Huron & Saginaw Bay
  Item 810042 $18.95

- Chart #75 N. Lake Huron & Straits of Mackinac
  Item 810050 $18.95

- BBA Chart Kit - Lake Michigan
  Item 690013 $54.95

- BBA Chart Kit - New Orleans to Panama City, FL
  Item 690020-10 $89.95

- BBA Chart Kit - Florida's West Coast and The Keys
  Item 690008-10 $84.95

- BBA Chart Kit - Jacksonville to Miami
  Item 690024-10 $54.95

- BBA Chart Kit - Norfolk to Jacksonville via ICW
  Item 690006-10 $73.95

- Chesapeake Bay Chart Book
  Item 699405 $42.50

The rest of the charts for the trip cover the rivers, canals and the New Jersey Coast. Many of the river charts are printed by the U.S. Army Corps of Engineers and can be ordered by writing to the district office in each region. A simple way of getting all the required charts is to order them from:

Marine Navigation
613 S. LaGrange Road
LaGrange, IL 60525
Phone Number: (708) 352-0606

The charts you will need are as follows:

	Marine Navigation
U.S. Army Corps of Engineers Charts:	1997 Prices

- *Charts of the Illinois Waterway* — $15.00

- *Upper Mississippi River Navigational Charts* — $18.00

- *Ohio River Navigational Charts - Cairo IL to Foster, KY* — $19.00

- *Tennessee River Navigational Charts* — $20.00

- *Tombigbee Waterway* — $39.00

- *Lower Black Warrior Waterway* — $36.00

NOAA Charts:

C & D canal to Buffalo, NY via New Jersey Shore, Hudson River and New York State Barge Canal System.

12304	$14.00
12311	$14.00
12316	$14.00
12324	$14.00
12327	$14.00
12341	$14.00
12343	$14.00
12347	$14.00
12348	$14.00
14786	$28.00
Total cost of all charts (1997 prices)	$887.60

2.   GPS

I strongly recommend GPS over Loran since Loran signals are very weak in the northern part of Lake Huron and Lake Michigan. GPS is also much quicker and more accurate. I started the trip with a built-in Loran and a hand-held GPS as a back up. I later converted the built-in Loran to a GPS; however, I still needed the hand-held back up when the new GPS broke down six months later.

3.   Depth Finder

You need a good depth finder especially in the intracoastal waterways and the Gulf of Mexico.

4.   Towing Insurance

We went from New Jersey to New Orleans without ever running aground. However, after running aground in Biloxi, Mississippi and then again on the West Coast of Florida intracoastal, I bought unlimited towing insurance from Boat/US for $88.00 per year. We only ran aground one more time on the trip, but the insurance easily paid for itself.

5.   Radar

I strongly recommend radar. The very first day of our trip was all fog as we ran 98 miles off the New Jersey coast. We also encountered fog on the morning of our second and third days out. We later experienced fog several times on Lake Erie and on some of the rivers. Radar was also helpful in determining how far off shore we were in the Great Lakes on clear days. Lastly, radar assists you to run in the rain and can help avoid thunderstorms.

6.   VHS Radio with Cell Phone Backup

We used our VHS radio for NOAA marine forecasts every day and to communicate with other boats and mariners. However, there were times when a marina didn't answer on VHS but we were able to get them on the cell phone. Since almost the entire trip is in sight of land, the cell phone works everywhere. We kept the cell phone in the salon plugged into the battery charger and carried it to the bridge when we were running.

7.   Auto Pilot

We did not have an autopilot, and we could not have used it very much if we did have one. The only places where you can use an autopilot are on the Great Lakes, Crossing the Gulf of Mexico and the New Jersey Coast. For the majority of the trip in rivers, canals and intracoastal waterways, your heading is constantly changing which makes it difficult to use an auto pilot system.

8.   Spare Props

We had spare props and needed them once, however, I understand from other boaters we met that we were lucky to only need them once. On a trip this long your chances of damaging a prop are pretty good, especially from floating debris.

9.   Shore Water and Two 50 FT. of Hoses

We had our boat outfitted with a shore water connection so when in dock we use fresh water from the dock that we can drink and we do not deplete our on-board supply. Our boat has two heads and a stall shower so we use lots of water. I found it a good idea to have two 50 ft. hoses, one to connect to the on board water system and one to wash the boat.

10. Shore Power Y-Adapter (Two 30 Amp Inlets to One 50 Amp Inlet)

We have two 30 amp, 110 volt electric inlets and two 50 ft. shore power cord sets. About 30% of the time we had to plug into a 50 amp outlet. The Y-adapter turned out to be very valuable.

11. Four-Step - Stepladder

We carried a four-step stepladder that folded flat for storage to help us get off the sides of our boat. With floating docks we could always get off the boat via a ladder to the swim platform. However, with fixed docks, we often had to get off the boat from the side. Unfortunately, there could be up to four feet between our deck and the dock. We simply lowered the stepladder onto the fixed dock and stepped right off onto the ladder.

12. Waterway Guides

In Chapter 3, I recommended that you purchase all the necessary waterway guides to help plan your trip, however, it is very important to bring them on the boat with you. You undoubtedly will go to some places on the trip that you didn't plan to and you will need the waterway guides for that. Every single time you go to a marina you will need the individual chart blowups in the waterway guides, which show the location of each marina.

13. Hand-Held Halogen Light

You will need a hand-held Halogen light that plugs into the cigarette lighter on the helm and has a 10-ft. long flexible cord. This light is invaluable when running at night and when docking or anchoring after dark. We started the trip without this light because we had a built-in searchlight. The searchlight turned out to be not nearly flexible enough or bright enough.

14. Navigation Tools

Besides a calculator and a set of parallel rulers, I would suggest a clipboard at the helm to hold a tablet with the days navigation data listed. You will need a good set of binoculars to read buoys and river mile markers. Lastly, I would suggest some large clips to put on the chart books at the helm so the pages don't blow.

15. Fenders and Fender Adjusters

You will need at least six fenders to be used when docking and in locks. In The Erie Canal you will buy straw bags to use as fenders so the locks don't chew up your good fenders. By the time you have finished the Erie Canal you will throw the straw bags away. We also recommend fender adjusters which allow you to raise and lower the fenders without untying the line.

16. TV

TV reception on board can be good, bad or non-existent depending on your situation. The best deal is an 18" satellite dish; however, this is fairly expensive. We had a TV aerial on the radar arch, which worked sometimes and not others. We also had a cable TV hookup on the boat. However, only about a third of the marinas we stayed at had cable service.

17. Clothing

We experienced temperatures from the 50's to the 90's on the trip although the great majority of the time we were able to wear shorts. We packed all of our clothes on board at the beginning of the trip and pretty much left it on board for the entire trip, even though we flew home three different times. I only needed a coat and tie twice, one at the Grand Hotel in Mackinac Island and once at the Commodore Palace Restaurant in New Orleans (both recommended). Laundry was not a problem since most of the marinas we stayed at had facilities.

18. Food and Supplies

We stocked the boat with food, drink, cleaning supplies, etc. at the beginning of the trip and replenished weekly as we traveled. Marina ship stores have a few items, but usually we had to go to the super market every week. Often the marina would have a courtesy car we could borrow to go shopping. If we were staying at a place for a while, we often rented a car for a few days (Enterprise Rent a Car will pick you up at the Marina).

New York to Buffalo
Hudson River and Erie Canal

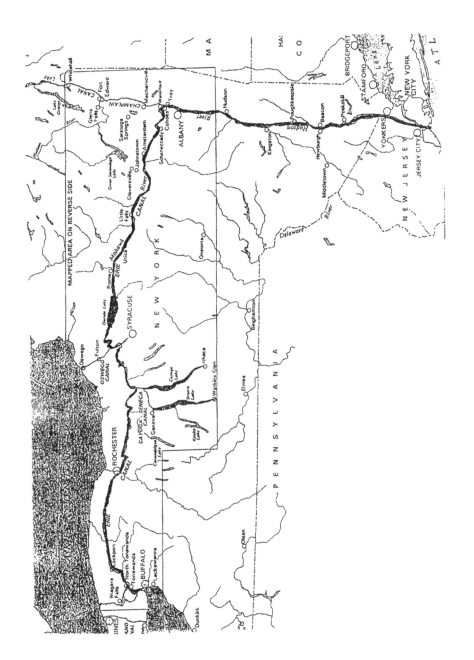

Destination	Distance (Statute Miles) Between Points	Cumulative
New York City, NY	0	0
Tarrytown, NY	30	30
Kingston, NY	58	88
Troy, NY	51	139
Fultonville, NY	48 (12 Locks)	187
Rome, NY	66 (8 Locks)	253
Baldwinsville, NY	58 (4 Locks)	311
Fairport, NY	74 (7 Locks)	385
Lockport, NY	74 (2 Locks)	459
Buffalo, NY	34 (3 Locks)	493

Charts Required:
NOHA Charts 12327, 12341, 12343, 12347, 12348, 14786

Water Way Guide:
Waterway Guide - Northern

NOTE: The destinations where the author stayed are shown in bold type and are described in the following chapter. The other destinations are listed as intermediate ports if a shorter cruising day is desired. Check the waterway guide for information on intermediate ports.

The Hudson River

The part of the Hudson that is on our trip goes from New York City to Troy New York beginning with The New York Harbor which is one of the most spectacular sites on the entire trip. Cruising up to the Statue of Liberty in your own boat is quite the thrill. This is obviously a photo-op to get everyone on deck for a photograph with the Statue of Liberty in the background. The Battery and the World Trade Center are also spectacular views from the water. In fact, the entire cruise up the Hudson alongside New York City is exciting.

As you cruise north, you pass one landmark after another such as the George Washington Bridge, the Palisades, Yonkers, Tappan Zee Bridge, Bear Mountain Bridge, West Point, Newburgh, N.Y., Poughkeepsie, N.Y., Hyde Park (Roosevelt's home), Kingston, N.Y., Albany, N.Y., and Troy, N.Y. The Hudson River has a current, which can be several knots, and after a rainstorm, floating debris can be a problem. For most of the way, from the Tappan Zee Bridge to Troy, the view is of beautiful rolling hills with large estates and farms coming down to the water. As you approach Albany from the South, with farms on either side of the river, the skyscrapers of the New York State Capital suddenly appear as you round a bend. A trip up the Hudson is worthwhile on its own.

New York City

New York City is a great place to spend several days of sight seeing. The United Nations, Broadway theaters, Lincoln Center, the New York Stock Exchange, museums, great restaurants and much much more. To have access to everything in Manhattan, one of the best marinas to stay in is the Newport Marina, located on the New Jersey side of the Hudson but only a 5-minute walk to the subway train to Manhattan. The Newport Marina is located about one half-mile north of the World Trade Center on the New Jersey side. All the marinas with transient slips are on the New Jersey side of the Hudson.

Newport Marina Phone: (201) 626-5550

Approach Depth	14'	**Diesel Fuel**	no
Dockside Depth	23'	**Mechanical Repairs**	yes
Accepts Transients	yes	**Ships Store**	yes
Dockside Power	30,50,100	**Showers**	yes
Dockside Water	yes	**Laundromat**	yes
Gasoline	no	**Restaurant**	yes

New York City to Tarrytown, N.Y.

The Hudson River Channel is well marked and the channel is quite deep varying from 15 feet to 175 feet deep. We ran into a substantial current since there had been a large rainstorm during that week so that we also had to dodge some floating debris. We had sunshine and enjoyed the beautiful scenery all the way. Immediately after passing under the Tappan Zee Bridge, you turn right into the Tarrytown Marina.

The crew of the Nittany Navy for the Hudson River and Erie Canal part of the trip was Buzz Mead and Bob and Charlotte Lande.

Tarrytown, N.Y

Tarrytown, New York was made famous by Washington Irving in his story *The Legend of Sleepy Hollow* which took place there. Washington Irving's house is outside of town and is open to the public. There is a nice restaurant right on the dock at the Tarrytown Marina.

Tarrytown Marina Phone: (914) 631-1300

Approach Depth	15'	**Diesel Fuel**	yes
Dockside Depth	15'	**Mechanical Repairs**	yes

Accepts Transients	yes	**Ships Store**	yes
Dockside Power	yes	**Showers**	yes
Dockside Water	yes	**Laundromat**	yes
Gasoline	yes	**Restaurant**	yes

Tarrytown to Troy, N.Y.

We started our trip from Tarrytown to Troy in dense fog. We used the radar to keep us in the middle of the river. The fog lifted just in time for us to see West Point, which is very imposing from the water; it looks like a massive fort built on the Cliffs on the west side of the river. We continued to see floating debris, which was a result of strong rainstorms during the last few days. Also, partially as a result of the rainstorms, we were bucking a strong 3-mph current. It took us 7.5 hours to do the 109 miles from Tarrytown to Troy, which was an average of 14 mph when we were cruising around 17 mph. We enjoyed the beautiful scenery and were amazed by how little boat traffic there was on this large river.

Troy, N.Y.

We stayed a the Troy Town dock which is a 1,000 ft. long floating dock in front of a 20 ft. high stone wall in down town Troy. From the dock you walk up stairs 20 feet to get to street level. The marina office is at street level, and that is where you buy straw bags for the Erie Canal. The straw bags are disposable fenders, and by the time you have made it to Buffalo they are ready to throw away. We had a 40-ft. boat so we bought 6 bags at $5.00 each and put them all on the starboard side. As it turned out, we were able to dock on the starboard side all but two times, when due to repairs on the lock, we were directed to dock on our port side. When this occurred, we used our permanent fenders instead of moving the straw bags. Across the street from the marina office is a microbrewery with a restaurant. We tried all six kinds of beer that they made.

Troy Town Dock Marina Phone: (518) 272-5341

Approach Depth	16'	Diesel Fuel	yes
Dockside Depth	21'	Mechanical Repairs	yes
Accepts Transients	yes	Ships Store	yes
Dockside Power	30,50	Showers	yes
Dockside Water	yes	Laundromat	yes
Gasoline	yes	Restaurant	yes

The Erie Canal

The Erie Canal was the first important waterway built in the United States. The Canal ran from Buffalo on Lake Erie across New York State to Troy and Albany on the Hudson so traffic could then go down the Hudson to New York City. By connecting the Great Lakes with the Atlantic Ocean the canal provided a route for manufactured goods to flow west and raw materials to flow east. The Canal was opened in 1825 at which time New York City was second to Philadelphia as a port and also as a city based on size. Ten years after the canal opened the Port of New York was larger than the Port of Philadelphia. Twenty years after the Canal opened, the city of New York was now the largest city in the United States.

The original Canal was 363 miles long. It was 28 feet wide at the bottom, 42 feet wide at the top, and 4 feet deep. It could carry boats that were 80 feet long and 15 feet wide with a draft of 3.5 feet. By 1862 the Canal had been enlarged several times. The present day Erie Canal was constructed near the old Canal and opened in 1918. Today the Canal has a depth of ten feet and all locks are 44.5 feet wide and 300 feet long. Even though it is called the New York State Barge Canal System, there are very few barges on the Canal. The overwhelming majority of boat traffic is recreational.

There are two routes to take on the Erie Canal depending on your boat's height above the water line. If your boat is 15.5 feet or less, you can take the Canal from Troy to Buffalo. If your boat is between 15.5 feet and 19 feet, you can take the Canal to Oswego, N.Y. on Lake Ontario, then take Lake Ontario to the Welland Canal, and the Welland Canal to Buffalo. We took the Canal to Buffalo, however, we had to take our radome down to get to 15.75 feet; and we actually scraped on the lowest bridge. If you take the Canal to Oswego on Lake Ontario, you will travel 180 miles and 31 locks rising to 420 feet elevation at Rome, N.Y. and descending to 246 feet on Lake Ontario. If you take the Canal to Buffalo, you will travel 363 miles and 36 locks rising to 572 feet on Lake Erie. The speed limit on the entire length of the Canal is 10 mph, except on Lake Oneida. Each lock takes about 25 minutes, so plan on four days to Oswego and six days to Buffalo. The cost is $15 per day; however, they had two-day tickets for $20, so we bought three tickets for $60.

Passing through a lock is an interesting experience. When approaching, you must stop at a safe distance and wait for the gates to open and a green light to come on before proceeding. If you have questions, you can talk to the Lockmaster on channel 10 on your VHF radio. Once the green light comes on, you proceed slowly (4 mph) into the lock and dock against the side of the lock. The lock will have lines approximately every 30 feet, which are connected at the top and hang over the side. Depending on the size of your boat, a crew member grabs hold of this line to hold the boat close to the wall of the lock. Since our boat was 40 feet long, we needed to hang onto two lines. These lines are very dirty, and you will need leather work gloves to handle the lines. After you have finished the Canal, you will throw these gloves away (or frame them!).

The locks can easily handle ten or more pleasure boats at a time. However, usually, you are in the lock by yourself or with two or three other boats. Since the speed limit is 10 mph the Lockmasters expect that if there are three boats in lock 4 they will all arrive at lock 5 together. The Lockmasters call ahead to the next lock to say that three boats have passed lock 4 so the next lock can be ready with the water at the correct level and the gates open when the three boats arrive. If one of those boats decides to speed at 20 mph the Lockmaster at the next lock will make the fast boat wait at the lock until the boats travelling at the speed limit are safely in the lock. Most of the locks are raising your boat, however, on the Buffalo route there are three lowering locks and there are eleven lowering locks on the Oswego route. Locks that raise your boat are easier because you come into the lock at the lowest level and you are protected from the wind. The wind can be a problem in Locks that lower your boat since you come into the lock with most of your boat above the lock walls. The Erie Canal locks range from 6 feet to 40.5 feet in vertical lift. All the locks work by gravity with the Lockmaster operating hydraulic valves to either raise or lower the water level in the lock.

Several weeks before you plan to go onto the Erie Canal it is a good idea to call the Canal System at (518) 471-5011 to make sure the Canal is fully operational. The Canal is generally closed from sometime in October to sometime in April due to ice. However, parts of the Canal can close for a period of time in spring and summer due to high water levels or other problems.

Troy to Fultonville

Lock No. 1 is at Troy on the Hudson River, so the Canal actually starts with Lock 2. Locks 2 through 6 are all quite close together; however, combined they lift your boat 170 ft. Lock No. 8 is in Schenectady, N.Y. We stopped for the night at Fultonville, N.Y., which is a few miles beyond Lock No. 12 and is 48 miles from Lock No. 2. We stayed at Poplars Inn and Marina, which is a motel with a restaurant and swimming pool. The dock is a floating dock on the side of the Canal with no electricity or water, however, it is the only place to stay on this part of the Canal. We used our generator to provide electricity. We had dinner at their restaurant and used the pool.

Fulton to Rome

The second day on the Erie Canal includes 66 miles and 8 Locks. Lock 17 with a 40.5 ft. lift is highest on the Erie Canal and is higher than any of the Panama Canal Locks. The scenery all along the Canal is very rural with farms, fields and woods. The Erie Canal Locks are beautifully maintained, freshly painted and most have flower gardens. At 10 mph, in this pastoral setting, you think you have gone back in time. Utica, N.Y. is between Locks 19 and 20. Our destination for the night is the Riverside Marina in Rome, N.Y., which is about 10 miles beyond Utica and is at an elevation of 420 ft. You cannot see the marina from the Canal; there is a sign with an arrow indicating that you turn left into what looks like a creek and go under a stone bridge after which you see the marina. There is an excellent restaurant in Rome called the Savoy and they will come and get you at the marina and bring you back after dinner.

Riverside Marina Phone: (315) 337-5720

Approach Depth	5'	**Diesel Fuel**	no
Dockside Depth	6'	**Mechanical Repairs**	yes
Accepts Transients	yes	**Ships Store**	no
Dockside Power	30,50	**Showers**	no
Dockside Water	yes	**Laundromat**	no
Gasoline	yes	**Restaurant**	no

Rome to Baldwinsville, N.Y.

After Rome you go through Locks 21 and 22 which lower your boat 50 feet to the level of Lake Oneida. Prior to these two locks, all the locks have been raising your boat. Lake Oneida is about 22 miles long and you follow channel markers across. There is no speed limit on the lake. There are marinas with fuel on either end of the lake. After the lake there is Lock 23 and then three rivers where the Oswego Canal joins the Erie Canal. If you are taking the Lake Ontario route to Buffalo, you leave the Erie Canal here and take the Oswego Canal north. If you are going to Buffalo all the way on the Erie Canal, you turn left at Three Rivers. After Three Rivers, the next town and Lock 24 is Baldwinsville, N.Y. Baldwinsville is a suburb of Syracuse. The total miles from Rome to Baldwinsville are 58. We stayed at Cooper's Marina, which is right on the Canal.

Cooper's Marina Phone: (315) 635-7371

Approach Depth	10'	**Diesel Fuel**	yes
Dockside Depth	10'	**Mechanical Repairs**	yes
Accepts Transients	yes	**Ships Store**	yes
Dockside Power	yes	**Showers**	yes

Dockside Water	yes	**Laundromat**	yes
Gasoline	yes	**Restaurant**	across the street

Baldwinsville to Fairport

From Baldwinsville to Fairport is 74 miles and 7 locks. The lowest bridge with less than 16 feet clearance is in this section. We got down to 15.75 feet by removing our radome, but we scraped the bridge. About 30 miles from Baldwinsville the Cayuga-Seneca Canal connects with the Erie Canal. If you wish to visit the Finger Lakes as a side trip, you would take this canal. Fairport is in between Lock 30 and Lock 32; there is no Lock 31. Fairport is a pretty town with a lift bridge and brick sidewalks on either side of the canal. There is no marina here and no fuel; however, their canal frontage is the nicest on the entire canal. We paid $7 for a 50 amp electric hookup and a water hookup for the night. There are several restaurants within short walking distance.

Fairport to Lockport, N.Y.

Fairport to Lockport is 74 miles and 2 locks. After going through Locks 32 and 33, the canal runs through the City of Rochester, N.Y. From Rochester to Lockport is more than 50 miles without any locks. We stayed at the Goehle Municipal Marina, which is a park with a docking facility. They only had 20-amp electric service and we require 50 amps, so we had to run our generator. We took a cab into town for dinner, which was unusual since the great majority of the time a nice restaurant was in walking distance or either the marina or restaurant provided a courtesy car.

Lockport to Buffalo, N.Y.

Locks 34 and 35 are in Lockport and are together in that
when you come out of Lock 34 you go right into Lock 35.
These locks end the actual canal since from here to the
Niagara River you are on the Tonawanda River. The distance
from Lockport to Buffalo is 34 miles with the last 9 miles on
the Niagara River. The Buffalo Harbor has a three-mile long
breakwater, which protects the harbor from lake waves. You
enter the breakwater at the northern end when coming from
the Niagara River and then into the Black Rock Lock and
Canal that bypasses the strong currents in the Niagara River.
The Canal has a 6-mph speed limit. At the end of the Canal
is the Erie Basin Marina, which is an excellent, large marina
surrounded by high-rise condos with water views.

The trip begins. Crew No. 1 — Bob Lande, Bick Remmey and Buzz Mead

The Statue of Liberty

New York Harbor

An Erie Canal Lock — going up

CHAPTER 5

Nittany Navy in an Erie Canal Lock

Buffalo to Detroit - Lake Erie

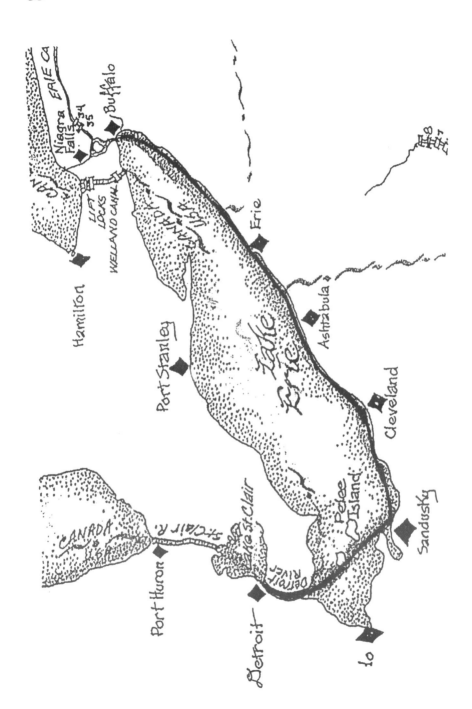

Destination	Distance (Statute Miles)	
	Between Points	Cumulative
Buffalo, NY	0	0
Dunkirk, NY	37	37
Erie, PA	45	82
Ashtabula, OH	48	130
Cleveland, OH	63	193
Cedar Point, OH	64	257
Put-In-Bay, OH	21	228
Detroit, MI	52	330

Charts Required:
Richardson's Chart Book and Cruising Guide - Lake Erie Edition

Water Way Guide:
Lakeland Boating Ports O'Call Lakes Erie & St. Clair

NOTE: The destinations where the author stayed are shown in bold type and are described in the following chapter. The other destinations are listed as intermediate ports if a shorter cruising day is desired. Check the waterway guide for information on intermediate ports.

Lake Erie

The tour of the "Rust Belt" from the water turned out to be much nicer than expected. Most marine facilities were very good and the skyline of Cleveland and Detroit are spectacular from the water. The marinas where we stayed in Buffalo, Erie and Cleveland were particularly nice, all with good restaurants on location. The resort areas of Cedar Point and Put-In-Bay were well worth the visit, independent of the boat trip. We made the Lake Erie trip with our friends Bill and Ann Gardner.

Lake Erie is the fourth largest of the Great Lakes and is 241 miles long and 56 miles wide at its widest point. The average depth is only 56 feet deep which accounts for the choppy water, which can build quickly with increase in wind speed. Because of the lake's position, it is subject to sudden afternoon squalls and thunderstorms. Due to this fact, I recommend that you plan your day to arrive at your destination by 3 p.m., which will beat most of the bad weather.

Lake Erie has some other problems that you may or may not encounter namely fog and floating debris. We encountered both. We had some dense fog on several days, and without our radar, we could not have moved. Lake Erie is fed by many rivers and streams and after a period of rain storms, particularly thunderstorms, tree branches and other floating debris are carried by the rivers and streams into the lake. We were on Lake Erie after a group of strong thunderstorms had gone through. As a result, we saw quite a lot of floating debris for several days.

On the trip from Buffalo to Cedar Point, I recommend that you cruise one to two miles off shore since the water is deep enough there and there is no reason to go out any further into the lake. From Cedar Point to Put-In-Bay and from there to the Detroit River, you are cruising across the lake so you should navigate by compass and GPS.

Our trip follows the southern shore, which starts out in New York and then follows the Pennsylvania shore and the Ohio shore to Cedar Point. Lake Erie is heavily traveled by commercial shipping, which you will rarely see when travelling close to shore. The southern shore of the lake has all the interesting destinations; whereas, the northern shore, which is Ontario, Canada, has no major cities, only small fishing villages.

Buffalo

Sights to see in Buffalo include the Allentown Historic District of beautiful 19th century mansions, one of which is the Theodore Roosevelt National Historic Site. Other attractions include the art and historical museums plus a naval museum with several World War II naval ships. Buffalo invented Buffalo Wings, so be sure to try these spicy chicken wings at the local restaurants.

Niagara Falls is only an hour drive from the marina area, and if you haven't seen it, it is worth a visit. The couple who did the Lake Erie part of our trip with us had never been to Niagara Falls, so we rented a car for the day and went to the Falls. It definitely qualifies as one of the natural wonders of the World.

Buffalo is one of the places where you might consider renting a car, not only for sight seeing, but also to get to the restaurants in the down town area. Crawdaddy's is a large restaurant right next to the Erie Basin Marina where we went twice because of good food and a great view.

Erie Basin Marina (Buffalo, New York)
Phone: (716) 842-4141

Approach Depth	29'	**Diesel Fuel**	yes
Dockside Depth	23'	**Mechanical Repairs**	yes

Accepts Transients	yes	**Ships Store**	yes
Dockside Power	30,50,100	**Showers**	yes
Dockside Water	yes	**Laundromat**	no
Gasoline	yes	**Restaurant**	short walk

Buffalo to Erie, Pennsylvania

(Richardson's Chart Book - Lake Erie Edition Pages 59, 58, 57, 55 and 73)

Our navigation plan was to follow the shoreline about two miles off from Buffalo to Erie. On of the nice things about cruising the Great Lakes is that you don't normally have to worry about running aground.

We made the 82-mile trip from Buffalo to Erie in 4 hours and 48 minutes. We left in a steady rain and had to dodge a lot of floating logs in the lake. By the time we got to the Lake Erie Yacht Club it was sunny.

Erie, Pennsylvania

The entrance to the Erie City port is on the east end of the Presque Isle Peninsula. This peninsula connects to the mainland at its western end and is open at its eastern end. The peninsula creates the Presque Isle Bay, which is 4.5 miles long and .5 miles wide. The city is on the southern shore of the Bay and the northern shore is a State Park. The park has a marina about a mile and a half west of the harbor entrance. There are no specific transient docks, however, the Dockmaster can usually find you a slip left open by one of the resident boats. No public transportation is available from the Park to the city.

Several marinas are located at the public dock downtown.

There are also several restaurants in the dock area and some of Erie's most interesting sights are within walking distance. We stayed at the Erie Yacht Club, which is several miles south from downtown on the Bay. To stay at the Erie Yacht Club, you must be a member of another Yacht Club and also make a reservation. The Erie Yacht Club is one of the finest Yacht Clubs in the United States with excellent facilities and a first class restaurant. The restaurant is closed on Monday.

Erie Yacht Club
(814) 453-4931 Office; (814) 456-9914 Gas Dock

R. D. McAllister & Son (Erie Public Dock)
Phone: (814) 452-3201

Approach Depth	7'	**Diesel Fuel**	yes
Dockside Depth	7'	**Mechanical Repairs**	yes
Accepts Transients	yes	**Ships Store**	yes
Dockside Power	30,50	**Showers**	yes
Dockside Water	yes	**Laundromat**	yes
Gasoline	yes	**Restaurant**	yes

Erie to Cleveland (*Richardson's Chart Book - Lake Erie Edition* Pages 24, 23, 22, 21, 20 and 39)

As with the previous day, our navigation plan was to cruise two miles off shore to Cleveland. We planned to make the 111 mile trip from Erie to Cleveland in one day, but the threat of early afternoon thunderstorms caused us to make an unplanned stop in Fairport, 24 miles short of Cleveland. We left Erie in sunshine, but we were actually rained on six different times that day with the last three after we were in Fairport. We had an interesting experience with our radar. We saw what looked like one large rainstorm up ahead, but the radar showed it was two distinct squalls. We set our course to go between the two and only experienced a few minutes of rain.

The next morning, we tried to leave Fairport at 9:00 a.m., but had to turn back because the fog was so dense. At 11:00 a.m. we followed a fishing boat out of the harbor into the lake where visibility was about one-half mile. Visibility was one mile by the time we got to Cleveland.

Cleveland

Cleveland, Ohio is 111 miles down the coast from Erie, Pennsylvania and 63 miles from Ashtabula, Ohio. Cleveland is a major city, which is now making a strong comeback, and a lot of the improvements are on the waterfront. The city waterfront is protected by a 5-mile long breakwater that creates a harbor. There are three entrances, one at the far northeast end, the main entrance at the Cuyahoga River, and the entrance at the far southeast end. We took the main entrance (page 39 *Richardson's Chart Book - Lake Erie Edition*). Immediately after passing underneath the Railroad Lift Bridge, turn to starboard into Old River and go approximately one mile to the Old River Yacht Club, which is on the right. The Old River Yacht Club is a new facility with a very nice restaurant and swimming pool area. If you are going to stay in Cleveland for a few days, I would recommend that you rent a car since there is so much to see and do there.

Along the Cuyahoga River are many nightclubs and restaurants. In downtown Cleveland near the stadium where the Cleveland Indians play is the Rock and Roll Hall of Fame. When we visited, we were surprised to find out that this is really a museum of American music, including Dixieland and

Country Music as well as Rock and Roll. On Euclid Avenue is the Old Arcade, a 19th-Century-enclosed mall of structural iron and glass, where elegant shops surround a central atrium on five balcony levels. A little further along Euclid is Cleveland's restored theater district, known as Playhouse Square.

Old River Yacht Club (Cleveland, Ohio)
Phone: (216) 281-6792

Approach Depth	10'	**Diesel Fuel**	no
Dockside Depth	10'	**Mechanical Repairs**	no
Accepts Transients	yes	**Ships Store**	no
Dockside Power	30,50	**Showers**	yes
Dockside Water	yes	**Laundromat**	yes
Gasoline	no	**Restaurant**	yes

Cleveland to Cedar Point - Sandusky Bay, Ohio
(*Richardson's Chart Book - Lake Erie Edition* Pages 20, 19, 18, 93, 97 and 98)

We continued to cruise about two miles off shore from Cleveland to Cedar Point. Our trip from Cleveland to Cedar Point was bumpy because our course was west and the winds were from the west at 15 knots. It was a sunny day and we made the 64-mile trip in a little over four hours.

Cedar Point

Next to Sandusky, Ohio is a peninsula that sticks about one mile into the lake with the Cedar Point Amusement Park on the end. Follow the Mosely Channel around the tip of Cedar Point to get to the Cedar Point Marina. The amusement park gate is next to the marina and there is free bus service for the

Cedar Point complex. Cedar Point is the roller coaster capital of the world with six roller coasters. Besides the amusement park, the complex includes two hotels, a sandy beach and several restaurants. The Cedar Point roller coasters are some of the scariest anywhere. One of them has 4 people across, standing up, and clamped in, of course. This roller coaster does a 360° loop where the people are upside down at the top of the loop.

Cedar Point Marina Phone: (419) 627-2334

Approach Depth	10'	**Diesel Fuel**	yes
Dockside Depth	8'	**Mechanical Repairs**	yes
Accepts Transients	yes	**Ships Store**	yes
Dockside Power	30,50	**Showers**	yes
Dockside Water	yes	**Laundromat**	yes
Gasoline	yes	**Restaurant**	yes

Cedar Point to Put-In-Bay (*Richardson's Chart Book - Lake Erie Edition* Pages 93, 92, 89, 88 and 105)

We originally had planned to go to Pelee Island, Canada from Cedar Point, which was only 38 miles away, but due north. The wind that day had shifted and was blowing from the north with 4 to 5 foot waves. As a result of the wind direction, we decided to go west to Put-In-Bay instead. This turned out to be a great decision, not only because we had a smooth ride, but because Put-In-Bay was such a great place.

Using *Richardson's Chart Book - Lake Erie Edition* the 21-mile trip from Cedar Point to Put-In-Bay is as follows. Starting on page 93, take the Moseley Channel to the end and then turn due north to the center of the south passage (page 92). Go west passing just south of south Bass Island (page 89).

Follow the West Coast of South Bass Island (page 88) to Put-In-Bay (page 105).

Put-In-Bay

Put-In-Bay is the only town on South Bass Island. The entire Island is recreational, and a great way to see it is to rent a bicycle, moped or golf cart. A must-see is the Perry Monument where park rangers tell the story of Perry's famous victory in the 1813 Battle of Lake Erie. The view from the top of the Monument is spectacular on a clear day, sometimes you can see the tall buildings of Detroit and Cleveland.

We rented a golf cart that held four people, two sitting forward and two sitting backward. We toured the entire island, which is very picturesque. Bill Gardner and my wife Jeri took a 12-minute plane ride in a replica of a 1935 Bi-plane with open cockpits. We had a fresh seafood dinner that night at the restaurant on the dock at the Boardwalk Marina and listened to the music of Eddie Boggs Band.

Boardwalk Marina (Put-In-Bay) Phone: (419) 285-6183

Approach Depth	8'	**Diesel Fuel**	no
Dockside Depth	8'	**Mechanical Repairs**	yes
Accepts Transients	yes	**Ships Store**	no
Dockside Power	30	**Showers**	no
Dockside Water	yes	**Laundromat**	no
Gasoline	yes	**Restaurant**	yes

Put-In-Bay to Detroit, Michigan (*Richardson's Chart Book - Lake Erie Edition* Pages 88, 15, 12, 122, 121, 120, 119, 118, and 117)

Our trip from Put-In-Bay to Detroit was on a beautiful sunny day with smooth seas. We left at 8:45 a.m. and arrived at 12:30 p.m.

From Put-In-Bay to the marinas north of downtown Detroit is 52 miles. When leaving Put-In-Bay, cruise past Rattlesnake Island and then set a northwest course for the Detroit River Channel (*Richardson's Chart Book - Lake Erie Edition* pages 15 and 12). The channel starts with a 44 ft. marker G "1 E" with coordinates of N. 41° 54.8' and E. 83° 06.5'. Follow the channel on chart pages 122, 121, 120, 119, 118 and 117. The marina where we stayed was Keans Detroit Yacht Harbor, which is a large marina with 400 slips and a large service department capable of every type of marine repair. We needed some repairs, so we were glad to be there.

Detroit, Michigan

If you plan to spend time in Detroit, I would recommend a rental car. Enterprise Car Rental will pick you up at the marina and take you to their offices to pick up your car. Places to see in Detroit include Greek Town, Renaissance Center, The Henry Ford Museum and Greenfield Village. Detroit also has some excellent museums and restaurants.

We stayed a total of four days in Detroit and we had an Enterprise rental car. We arrived on a Monday and went to Greek Town for dinner that night. Tuesday we went sight seeing at The Henry Ford Museum and Greenfield Village which is a collection of the actual homes and work places of famous inventors; Henry Ford's birthplace and the original Ford Motor Co. building, Thomas Edison's Menlo Park Laboratory, and the Wright Brothers' home and bicycle shop, etc. Wednesday, we drove Ann and Bill Gardner to the

Detroit Airport for their flight back to Philadelphia. Thursday, we picked up our next crew, Jim and Nancy Hoffman who were flying in from Colorado. The repairs we needed done were completed on Thursday and we were ready to start the next leg of our trip on Friday.

Keans Detroit Yacht Harbor (Detroit, Michigan)
Phone: (313) 822-4500

Approach Depth	8'	**Diesel Fuel**	no
Dockside Depth	7'	**Mechanical Repairs**	yes
Accepts Transients	yes	**Ships Store**	yes
Dockside Power	30	**Showers**	yes
Dockside Water	yes	**Laundromat**	yes
Gasoline	yes	**Restaurant**	no

Nittany Navy at the Erie, Pennsylvania Yacht Club

Harbor at Put-in-Bay

Renaissance Center in Detroit

Detroit to Mackinac Island – Lake Huron

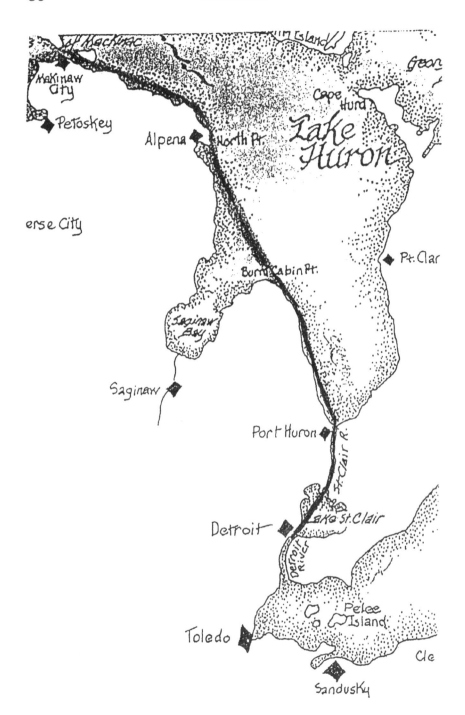

Distance (Statute Miles)

Destination	Between Points	Cumulative
Detroit, MI	0	0
Port Huron, MI	50	50
Harbor Beach, MI	55	105
Harrisville, MI	55	160
Rogers City	49	209
Cheboygan, MI	42	251
Mackinac Island, MI	14	265

Charts Required:
Richardson's Chart Book and Cruising Guide - Lake Erie Edition
Chart #74 S. Lake Huron & Saginaw Bay
Chart #75 N. Lake Huron & Straits of Mackinac

Water Way Guide:
Lakeland Boating Ports O'Call Lake Huron

NOTE: The destinations where the author stayed are shown in bold type and are described in the following chapter. The other destinations are listed as intermediate ports if a shorter cruising day is desired. Check the waterway guide for information on intermediate ports.

Detroit to Port Huron
Richardson's Chart Book and Cruising Guide – Lake Erie Edition Pages 117, 113, 112, 114, 110, 109, 108 and 123

We left Detroit at 9 o'clock and arrived at Port Huron at 12:15 p.m. You follow the Detroit River to Lake St. Clair. After crossing the lake following the clearly marked channel, you enter the St. Clair River. The St. Clair River takes you to Port

Huron, which is the entrance to Lake Huron. We had a beautiful, sunny day and the ride was very smooth. We stayed at the municipal marina in Port Huron.

Port Huron

Besides the Municipal Marina, Port Huron also has several private marinas and a yacht club all on the Black River. Restaurants and shopping are walking distance from the Municipal Marina. We had an excellent dinner at the Edison Inn which was not in walking distance; however, they sent a courtesy car to take us to and from the restaurant. Sarinia, Canada is located across the St. Clair River from Port Huron. Sarinia is an industrial city much larger than Port Huron. If you would prefer to stay in Canada, Sarinia has good marina facilities; however, you will have to go through customs.

Municipal Marina Phone: (810) 984-9745

Approach Depth	28'	**Diesel Fuel**	yes
Dockside Depth	15'	**Mechanical Repairs**	no
Accepts Transients	yes	**Ships Store**	no
Dockside Power	30,50	**Showers**	yes
Dockside Water	yes	**Laundromat**	yes
Gasoline	yes	**Restaurant**	yes

Lake Huron

Lake Huron is the second largest of the Great Lakes next to Lake Superior. It is different from the other lakes in that there are no large cities on the Lake. The character of the lake is very rural with all ports being small towns or villages. Since our route followed the Michigan shore, we usually were within several miles of shore except when crossing Saginaw

Bay. The lake is quite deep so that even though we were close to shore we were usually running in 40 feet of water or more. As you travel north, the temperature drops so that the temperature in Mackinac Island is significantly cooler than Port Huron. We spent the 4th of July on Mackinac Island and you needed a sweater in the morning and evening. We found the Loran signals to be very weak in the northern part of the lake, however, the GPS signals were strong.

Port Huron to Harbor Beach
Chart #74 S. Lake Huron & Saginaw Bay

The trip from Port Huron to Harbor Beach took us 3.5 hours to travel the 55 miles running along the Michigan shoreline. It was a sunny day but quite windy. A storm was predicted to hit our area in mid-afternoon, so we left at 8:00 a.m. and arrived at 11:30 a.m. After gassing up at the state marina in Harbor Beach, we moved our boat to our slip and were caught by a gust of wind that slammed our boat into the dock. Unfortunately, there was a piece of metal on the dock that punctured our hull about 2 feet above the water line. Later that day, we were able to get a diver to patch the hole in our hull with epoxy.

Harbor Beach

Harbor Beach is a small town with a state marina, which is protected by a sea wall. This was the first of a number of marinas that we stayed in that were run by the State of Michigan. These marinas are new and offer excellent facilities at a very reasonable price (0.75 cents per foot). The only bad news is that they do not take reservations so it is first come-first serve. These marinas can fill up especially on summer weekends, so I recommend you get there before 2:00 p.m.

Harbor Beach Marina   Phone: (517) 479-9707

Approach Depth	10'	Diesel Fuel	yes
Dockside Depth	10'	Mechanical Repairs	no
Accepts Transients	yes	Ships Store	yes
Dockside Power	30,50	Showers	yes
Dockside Water	yes	Laundromat	yes
Gasoline	yes	Restaurant	.5 miles

Harbor Beach to Harrisville

Chart #75 S. Lake Huron & Saginaw Bay and Chart #75 N. Lake Huron & Straits of Mackinac

The storm that was predicted veered off and we were surprised to have good weather for our trip to Harrisville. We left the Harbor Beach Marina and went straight out into the lake for about 6 miles after which we went on a GPS course direct to Harrisville. Harrisville's coordinates are N 44° 39.5' and W 83° 17'. This course takes you across the mouth of Saginaw Bay, and you are out of sight of land most of the trip. It was a beautiful day with smooth water and we made the trip in 3.5 hours.

Harrisville

Harrisville is a neat, clean town with a population of around 700. The Harrisville City Dock is another state-run marina with excellent new facilities and a 75-cent per foot slip fee. We had dinner in a very nice German restaurant that sent a courtesy car to the marina to bring us to the restaurant. Harrisville is very typical of the Lake Huron Port towns.

Harrisville City Dock   Phone: (517) 724-5242

Approach Depth	12'	Diesel Fuel	yes

Dockside Depth	5'	Mechanical Repairs	no
Accepts Transients	yes	Ships Store	no
Dockside Power	30,50	Showers	yes
Dockside Water	yes	Laundromat	yes
Gasoline	yes	Restaurant	.5 miles

Harrisville to Cheboygan
Chart #75 N. Lake Huron & Straits of Mackinac

The good weather continued with lots of sun and smooth water. We made the 91-mile trip in less that 7 hours including a gas stop at Rogers City. We left Harrisville and went about 5 miles out into the lake where we turned north and set our GPS course to Thunder Bay Island which has a 63 foot tower with a horn. Your next GPS waypoints are Middle Island, which has a 78-foot tower, and the Presque Island Lighthouse, which is 123 feet high. The next waypoint was Rogers City where we stopped for gas and then onto Cheboygan.

Cheboygan

The reason that we continued on to Cheboygan instead of staying overnight in Rogers City was because of the Mackinac Island Marina situation. The Mackinac Island Marina is run by the State of Michigan and is the only marina on the island. This marina has only 65 slips and you cannot make a reservation. Also, this is the busiest marina in Michigan. To get into the marina, you must be in the Mackinac Island Harbor in view of the people in the marina office. You talk to them on your VHF radio and they assign a wait list number. We arrived in the Mackinac Island Harbor at 8:00 a.m. and were given a wait list number of 14. We got into the marina at 1:00 p.m. This occurred on July 2nd; however, most other summer days would not be that crowded.

Cheboygan is in the south channel portion of the Mackinac Straits. After entering the south channel, you follow the Cheboygan Channel into the Cheboygan River. All the marinas are on the Cheboygan River. On entering the river, you pass the 290 foot-long Coast Guard Cutter, *Mackinac*, which is docked there. This boat is used to break up ice in late fall and early spring. We stayed at Walstrom Marina and had a good dinner at the Boathouse Restaurant, which is on the river.

Walstrom Marina Phone: (616) 627-7105

Approach Depth	25'	**Diesel Fuel**	no
Dockside Depth	15'	**Mechanical Repairs**	yes
Accepts Transients	yes	**Ships Store**	yes
Dockside Power	30,50	**Showers**	no
Dockside Water	yes	**Laundromat**	no
Gasoline	no	**Restaurant**	yes

Cheboygan to Mackinac Island
Chart #75 Lake Huron and Straits of Mackinac

We left Cheboygan at 7:00 a.m. in light rain. We cruised up the center of the South Channel for about 7 miles, then followed the shoreline of Bois Blanc Island to the West End. We continued past Round Island to Mackinac Island. We arrived at Mackinac Island Harbor at 8:00 a.m. and immediately called the marina office on our VHF radio. We were number 14 on the waiting list.

Mackinac Island

After we got our name on the waiting list, we tied up at a coal dock to wait. Since it was raining, the girls stayed on the boat to listen on the radio for us to be called. Jim Hoffman and I put on our rain gear and walked into town. At 1:00 p.m. we were called to come into the marina and the sun came out. We were put into a 40-ft. slip with a 20-ft. boat already in the slip so that our 40-ft. boat stuck out by 20 ft. The Fourth of July Holiday is the busiest time of the year for the busiest marina in the State of Michigan. By rafting up and doubling up, I think they got about 100 boats into their 65-slip marina.

Mackinac Island, which is only reachable by ferry or your own boat, is a great place to visit. There are no automobiles allowed on the Island, so all transportation is by horse and carriage or bicycle. The island is approximately three miles long and two miles wide. There is a road around the perimeter of the island, which is 8 miles long. We rented bicycles one morning and rode around the entire island. There is only one village on the island, which is located around the harbor. The architecture is Victorian, and with no automobiles, it looks like the 1890's. The town has several hotels and many restaurants and shops. Based on the number of fudge shops, Mackinac Island must be the fudge capital of the world.

At one end of the village is the world famous Grand Hotel, which was built in 1887 and is the world's largest wooden hotel. The front porch of the hotel is more than 800 ft. long and has many pillars with flower boxes planted with red geraniums in between. The hotel sits on a hill with a beautiful view and there are hundreds of white rocking chairs on the front porch. Sitting on the porch, you look down on beautiful gardens and lawn, which run down to the water. People not staying at the hotel can have dinner there, however, a coat and tie is required. After dinner they have dancing in an elegant ballroom with a big band.

On the hill above the village is Fort Mackinac, which took part in the war of 1812. The Fort is open to the public and is very worthwhile to visit. Men in period costumes reenact the life in the Fort in the 18th century. We stayed on Mackinac Island for 4 days, including the 4th of July. It is interesting to note that the island is so far north that it didn't get dark enough for the fireworks until 10:00 p.m.

Mackinac Island Marina Phone: (906) 847-3561

Approach Depth	10'	**Diesel Fuel**	no
Dockside Depth	8'	**Mechanical Repairs**	no
Accepts Transients	yes	**Ships Store**	no
Dockside Power	30	**Showers**	yes
Dockside Water	yes	**Laundromat**	yes
Gasoline	yes	**Restaurant**	close by

Mackinac Island Marina, Crew No. 3 — Bick and Jeri Remmey,
Nancy and Jim Hoffman

Mackinac Island has no cars

Mackinac Island to Chicago – Lake Michigan

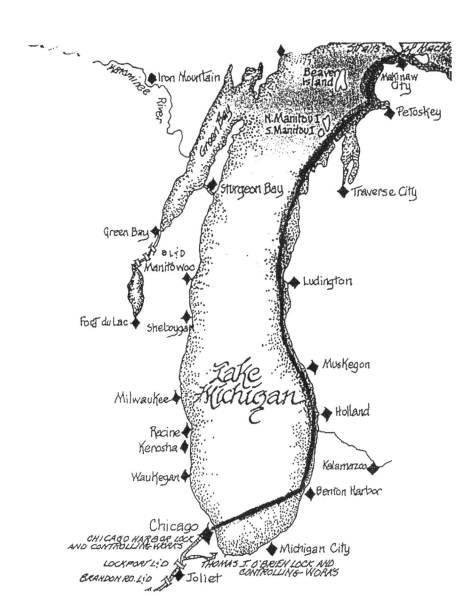

Iron Mountain

Menominee River

Green Bay

Beaver Island

Mackinaw City

Petoskey

N.Manitou I
S.Manitou I

Straits

St.Mach

Sturgeon Bay

Traverse City

Green Bay

BLVD

Manitowoc

Ludington

Fond du Lac

Sheboygan

Muskegon

Milwaukee

Lake Michigan

Holland

Racine

Kenosha

Kalamazoo

Waukegan

Benton Harbor

Chicago

CHICAGO HARBOR LOCK
AND CONTROLLING WORKS

Michigan City

LOCKPORT L:D

THOMAS J. O'BRIEN LOCK AND
CONTROLLING WORKS

BRANDON RD. L:D

Joliet

| Destination | Distance (Statute Miles) | |
	Between Points	Cumulative
Mackinac Island, MI	0	0
Petoskey, MI	50	50
Charlevoix, MI	15	65
Frankfort, MI	67	132
Pentwater, MI	54	186
Holland, MI	60	246
Benton Harbor, MI	41	287
Chicago, IL	53	340

Charts Required:
BBA Chart Kit – Lake Michigan

Waterway Guide:
Lakeland Boating Ports O' Call - Lake Michigan

NOTE: The destinations where the author stayed are shown in bold type and are described in the following chapter. The other destinations are listed as intermediate ports if a shorter cruising day is desired. Check the waterway guide for information on intermediate ports.

Lake Michigan

Lake Michigan is 320 miles long and varies between 50 and 80 miles wide. The lake is quite deep with depths up to 600 feet. The summer winds are from the West and afternoon thunderstorms are common. As a result of this, I recommend starting your cruise early enough to be in port before 3:00 p.m. Our cruise took us along the Eastern Shore of the lake, which has sandy beaches, and miles and miles of large sand dunes. There are many small lakes behind the dunes, which are connected to Lake Michigan with canals, so that the small lakes become safe harbors.

Mackinac Island to Petoskey
BBA Chart Kit – Lake Michigan Pages 33, 36, 32 and 30

We left Mackinac Island at 7:00 a.m. on a sunny day with high winds. Unfortunately, our course for the first 25 miles was due west which was right into the wind. We had 6-ft. waves and we pounded into them for two hours since we had to slow down. This actually turned out to be the roughest weather we encountered on the entire trip. One member of our crew got sick.

When leaving Mackinac Island you come out of the harbor and head directly for the bridge that connects upper and lower Michigan and is the official border between Lake Huron and Lake Michigan. After passing under the bridge, follow a course of 275 for 20 miles to the White Shoal Light, which is 125 feet high. At the light, turn south on a course of 190 for 5 miles to the Grays Reef Light, which is 82 feet high. At this light, change course to 160 and head for the coast. When you get within 2 miles of the coast, follow the coastline into Little Traverse Bay to Petoskey. It is interesting to note how important wind direction is. Our first two hours into the wind were very rough; however, when we turned south, the ride improved, and when we turned east going into Little Traverse Bay with the wind at our back, it was actually smooth. We arrived in Petoskey at 10:30 a.m.

Petoskey

Petoskey is at the eastern end of Little Traverse Bay. We stayed at the municipal dock, which is about one-half mile

from downtown.   The Little Traverse Historical Society
Museum is adjacent to the marina.   This museum has a
Hemingway section since Ernest Hemingway lived in Petoskey
when he was young. We had dinner at Hemingway's favorite
restaurant the Park Garden Café. Jim and Nancy Hoffman,
who had been with us since Detroit, left us in Petoskey to fly
home to Colorado.   Len and Kathryn Doherty, who are
neighbors of ours in Yardley, Pennsylvania, arrived several
hours later. The Dohertys went with us to Chicago.

Petoskey Municipal Marina Phone: (616) 347-6691

Approach Depth	10'	**Diesel Fuel**	no
Dockside Depth	9'	**Mechanical Repairs**	no
Accepts Transients	yes	**Ships Store**	no
Dockside Power	30	**Showers**	yes
Dockside Water	yes	**Laundromat**	no
Gasoline	yes	**Restaurant**	.5 miles

Petoskey to Charlevoix
BBA Chart Kit – Lake Michigan Page 30

Charlevoix is only 15 miles from Petoskey, so the whole trip
was only one hour. Since the two towns are so close together,
you could easily skip one or the other. We thought both
towns were interesting and worthy of a visit.

Charlevoix, Michigan

Charlevoix is probably the prettiest town on the eastern shore
of Lake Michigan. Entering from Lake Michigan you pass
through a short canal with houses and restaurants on either
side, then under a drawbridge and into a small lake. The
small lake is called Round Lake and has a municipal marina.

Round Lake connects to Lake Charlevoix which is much larger. Our marina, the Northwest Marina, was on Lake Charlevoix.

Charlevoix is the home of the Belvedere Club which was built before prohibition. This private club includes several hundred large, wooden summer homes of the 1920's vintage plus a private golf course, tennis courts, marina and beach area only for members. There are a number of good restaurants there. Two that we especially liked were the Grey Gables, next to the Belvedere Club, and the Weather Vane Restaurant which is next to the drawbridge.

Northwest Marina   Phone: (616) 547-5552

Approach Depth	8'	**Diesel Fuel**	no
Dockside Depth	8'	**Mechanical Repairs**	yes
Accepts Transients	yes	**Ships Store**	yes
Dockside Power	30,50	**Showers**	yes
Dockside Water	yes	**Laundromat**	yes
Gasoline	no	**Restaurant**	.5 miles

Charlevoix to Frankfort
BBA Chart Kit – Lake Michigan Pages 30, 29, 27, 26 and 25

When NOAA issues a "small craft warning" we don't go. However, when NOAA issues a "small craft advisory" we often go if the wind is at our back. On the day we planned to go to Frankfort, we had a "small craft advisory" with south winds 15 knots and we were headed south so we did not go. The winds were forecasted to change to northwest the next day. The next day, the wind did shift to the northwest and the "small craft advisory" still existed so we went to Frankfort. We had 2 to 4 ft. waves but not a bad ride and it got smoother as we ran.

The course from Charlevoix to Frankfort follows the Michigan Coast South Crossing over the mouth of Grand Traverse Bay past the Grand Traverse Bay Light (50-feet high). You continue to follow the coast south to the North Manitou Shoals Light, which is 79 feet high. You then take the Manitou Passage between North and South Manitou Island and the Michigan Coast. The course is 245 and the passage is 12 miles. Next set a course of 200 which will bring you back to the Michigan shoreline in about 15 miles and follow the shoreline from there to Frankfort.

Frankfort

The large dunes on the Michigan Coast start north of Frankfort including some as high as 480 feet. As you come into Frankfort from the water you go into a canal cut through the dunes into a lake behind the dunes which forms a safe harbor. The lake is called Betsy Lake and the town and marinas are located on your left as you come through the canal. We stayed at the Jacobson Marina, which was one of the best marinas that we stayed at on the entire trip. This marina had a very nice built-in picnic table and benches plus a gas grill for each two slips. The main street in the town is only one block away with some nice shops and restaurants. We had dinner at the Frankfort Hotel, which featured German food and an extensive wine cellar.

Jacobson Marina Phone: (616) 382-9131

Approach Depth	18'	**Diesel Fuel**	yes
Dockside Depth	12'	**Mechanical Repairs**	yes
Accepts Transients	yes	**Ships Store**	yes

Dockside Power	30,50	Showers	yes
Dockside Water	yes	Laundromat	yes
Gasoline	yes	Restaurant	yes

Frankfort to Holland

BBA Chart Kit – Lake Michigan Pages 21, 19, 15, 12 and 14

We had originally planned to go from Frankfort to Pentwater to stay the night and then onto Holland. However, since we had spent an extra day in Charlevoix, we decided to make it up by going from Frankfort to Holland in one day. The four of us had airplane tickets home from Chicago and we didn't want to cut our time in Chicago short. The other reason for our decision was that the weather was beautiful and the lake was flat.

We simply followed the coastline 2 to 3 miles off the whole way. However, I always program our waypoints into the GPS, which gives you *miles to go* and *time to go*, as well as course corrections at the end. In this case, I programmed both Pentwater and Holland since we planned to stop in Pentwater for gas. We left Frankfort at 8:00 a.m. and were in Pentwater by noon. We arrived in Holland by 4:00 p.m. having traveled 114 miles that day.

Holland

Holland is another town on a lake behind the sand dunes. After coming through the short canal into the lake, you turn right into the Eldean Shipyard, which is a very nice marina with a gourmet restaurant overlooking all the boats. The town of Holland is located at the other end of Lake Macatawa, which is 5 miles long. Holland was originally settled by the Dutch and is famous for their annual Tulip Festival in May.

On the outskirts of town are two wooden shoe factories and a tulip farm that you can visit.

Eldean Shipyard Marina (616) 335-5843

Approach Depth	20'	Diesel Fuel	yes
Dockside Depth	17'	Mechanical Repairs	yes
Accepts Transients	yes	Ships Store	yes
Dockside Power	30,50	Showers	yes
Dockside Water	yes	Laundromat	yes
Gasoline	yes	Restaurant	yes

Holland to Benton Harbor

BBA Chart Kit – Lake Michigan Pages 12, 10 and 11

The trip from Holland to Benton Harbor is only 41 miles down the Michigan coastline. We arrived in time for lunch. The weather continued to be good.

Benton Harbor

Benton Harbor and its neighboring town of St. Joseph are industrial towns, and the only reason for going there is that the trip across the lake to Chicago is only 53 miles. You can skip this port and go to Chicago directly from Holland, but that trip is 90 miles long. Since we didn't know what the weather would be like, we opted for the shorter trip. I'm sure that one of these towns has a nice restaurant, but the one we went to was mediocre. In retrospect this would have been a good place to have dinner on board.

Riverview 1000 Marina (616) 927-4471

Approach Depth	6'	Diesel Fuel	yes
Dockside Depth	6'	Mechanical Repairs	yes

Accepts Transients	yes	**Ships Store**	yes
Dockside Power	30,50	**Showers**	yes
Dockside Water	yes	**Laundromat**	yes
Gasoline	yes	**Restaurant**	Taxi ride

Benton Harbor to Chicago

BBA Chart Kit – Lake Michigan Pages 10, 2, 4 and 5

We made the 53-mile crossing from Benton Harbor to Chicago in 3 hours. The weather continued to be good and we had a smooth ride. We could see the tops of the Chicago skyscrapers from 20 miles out; in particular the Sears Tower. The Chicago skyline from the lake is a spectacular sight. We went on a course of 255 for 45 miles from Benton Harbor to a waypoint (page 4) N 41° 51.1' and W 87° 36.5'. From there we went on a course of 240 for 8 miles to the entrance of the Burnham Park Harbor. The coordinates of the harbor entrance are N 41° 51.1' and W 87° 36.5'.

Chicago

We stayed at the Burnham Park Municipal Marina, which I strongly recommend due to its location. This marina is run by the City of Chicago and is quite large. They do not have any transient slips as such, however, if you call them several days in advance, they will assign you a slip that will be empty during your stay. The marina is located in a protected body of water with a small plane airport on the lakeside and the McCormick Center and Soldiers Field on the city side. Adjacent to the North end of the marina is the Adler Planetarium, the Shedd Aquarium and the Field Museum of Natural History. Also in front of the Aquarium is a place to get tour buses of the city and a very busy taxi stand.

Chicago has so much to do, however, we were only there for three days. We visited all the museums that were in walking distance and we took the open trolley tour of the city. We had dinner at Georgettes, which is a great steak restaurant. We also had dinner at Rosebuds, a good Italian restaurant. We didn't have time to eat at the 300 other good restaurants in Chicago.

Burnham Park Municipal Harbor Phone: (312) 747-7009

Approach Depth	20'	**Diesel Fuel**	yes
Dockside Depth	15'	**Mechanical Repairs**	no
Accepts Transients	yes	**Ships Store**	no
Dockside Power	30,50	**Showers**	yes
Dockside Water	yes	**Laundromat**	yes
Gasoline	yes	**Restaurant**	no

Marina at Frankfort, Michigan

Marina in downtown Chicago next to Soldiers Field

Entering the Chicago River from Lake Michigan

Chicago to the Tenn-Tom Canal
Illinois, Mississippi, Ohio and
Tennessee Rivers

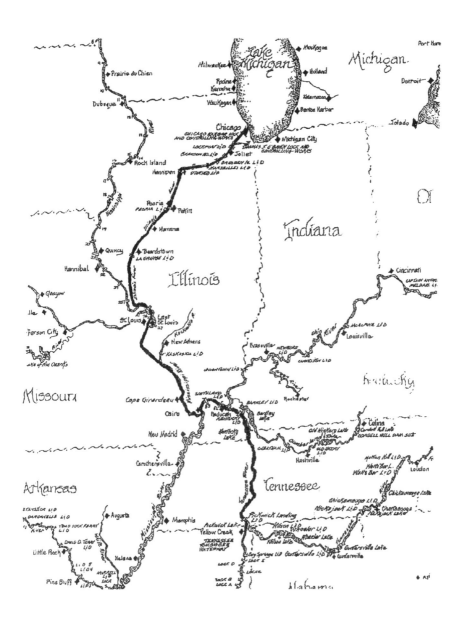

Destination	Distance (Statute Miles) Between Points	Cumulative
Chicago, IL	0	0
Wilmington, IL	55 (2 locks)	55
Henry, IL	78 (3 locks)	133
Pekin, IL	43 (1 lock)	176
Browning, IL	56	232
Naples, IL	32 (1 lock)	264
Portage de Sioux, MO	71	335
Ste. Genevieve, MO	90 (2 locks)	425
Cairo, IL (Anchorage)	121	546
Grand River, KY	83 (3 locks)	629
Buchanan, TN	43	672
Waverly, TN	49	721
Saltillo, TN	57	788
Iuka, MS	47 (1 lock)	825

Charts Required:

U.S. Army Corps of Engineers Charts
     Charts of the Illinois Waterway
     Upper Mississippi River Navigational Charts
     Ohio River Navigational Charts – Cairo, Illinois to
          Foster, Kentucky
     Tennessee River Navigational Charts

Waterway Guide:

Quimby's Cruising Guide

NOTE: The destinations where the author stayed are shown in bold type and are described in the following chapter. The other destinations are listed as intermediate ports if a shorter cruising day is desired. Check the waterway guide for information on intermediate ports.

The Illinois Waterway

The Illinois Waterway starts at Lake Michigan with the Chicago River and the Calumet River, which join the Des Plaines River and then the Kankakee River to form the Illinois River near Joliet, Illinois. The Illinois River flows southeast to the Mississippi River at Grafton, Illinois about 20 miles north of St. Louis. The Illinois Waterway has seven locks, which will lower your boat from 580 feet elevation at Lake Michigan to 433 feet elevation at the junction with the Mississippi River. All the locks are 110 feet wide by 600 feet long. Red nun buoys are located on the left edge of the channel and black can buoys are located on the right edge of the channel when proceeding downstream. An additional aid to navigation is the mile markers, which start at Mile 1 at the Mississippi River and go to mile 333 at Lake Michigan.

Chicago to Wilmington, Illinois

There are a number of fixed bridges on the Illinois Waterway however the two lowest are a 17 foot clearance on the Chicago River and a 19 foot clearance at mile 302 after the Calumet and Chicago Rivers come together. If you can clear the 17 foot bridge you can take the Chicago River through downtown Chicago from Lake Michigan otherwise you must take the Calumet River from Lake Michigan. In both cases you still have to clear the 19 foot bridge. I recommend you start this trip early since the speed limit is 6 mph all through Chicago and there are a number of lift bridges that you have to wait for. After coming through the city of Chicago, about 42 miles from the lake is the Lockport Lock at Mile 291. The next lock is only 5 miles away which is the Brandon Road Lock at Mile 286 Wilmington, Illinois and the Haborside Marina are at Mile

273.7. You are now travelling through rural farm areas. This 55-mile trip took us 8 hours.

Harborside Marina Phone: (815) 476-2254

Accepts Transients	yes	**Mechanical Repairs**	yes
Dockside Power	30,50	**Ships Store**	yes
Dockside Water	yes	**Showers**	yes
Gasoline	yes	**Laundromat**	no
Diesel Fuel	yes	**Restaurant**	yes

Wilmington, Illinois to Henry, Illinois

I recommend that you get an early start on this day even though you will be able to go at cruising speeds most of the time. There are three locks where there can be considerable delays. On the Erie Canal the boat traffic is recreational, so there are very seldom long delays at locks. However, the major traffic on the Illinois Waterway is barge traffic and they have the preference at locks. The first lock after Wilmington is the Dresden Island Lock at Mile 271.5. We arrived at this lock with a 1,100-ft. long tow headed in our direction and waiting for a tow that was in the lock coming the opposite direction. After about 15 minutes the upstream tow cleared the lock and the 1,100-ft. tow started pushing into the 600-ft. long lock. When 600 feet of barges were in the lock, they disconnected the remaining 500 feet of barges and then moved them sideways so they could push the 500-ft. train of barges into the lock parallel to the 600 feet of barges already in the lock. The tugboat was at the end of the 500-ft. barge train so that the tow now filled the entire space of 110-feet wide by 600-ft. long inside the lock. Once the tow was lowered to the new level, it pushed out of the lock and then had to be reassembled. They then closed the gates and raised the water so we could pass through the Lock. This entire process took three hours.

This turned out to be the longest delay that we had at any lock on the entire trip. However, we had a 5-hour delay at a lock on the St. Lawrence Seaway on a previous trip when large ships were coming from both directions and had priority over pleasure boats. The typical tow of less than 600 feet in length can get through the lock in 30 minutes because it does not have to disassemble and reassemble. The Illinois River and the Mississippi River have very heavy barge traffic where you see a tow either going upstream or downstream every 10 to 15 minutes. When you see a tow, you contact them on your VHF radio to ask which side they want you to pass them on. The western river's whistle signals when boats are passing are - one blast means "I intend to leave you on my port side", and two blasts means " I intend to leave you on my starboard side". It is the common practice to not blow the whistle but to ask the tug captain on the radio, which he prefers "one or two whistles?" All tows move at 6 mph, so slow down to 8 mph when passing them.

The section of the trip covered in this chapter (Chicago to the Tenn-Tom Canal) had some special problems, which I will discuss later. For this reason my crew for this section of the trip was Charlie Frame who was an experienced captain and had captained his own boat extensively on the Inland Waterway. After my wife Jeri and I came through Chicago, we left our boat at a marina on the Illinois River and flew home. Two months later Charlie and I flew back to Chicago, picked up the boat at the marina and resumed the trip.

The trip from Wilmington to Henry, Illinois is 78 miles long and includes 3 locks. The second lock is the Marseilles Lock, which is at Mile 244.6. The third lock is the Starved Rock Lock at Mile 231. We did not have any delays at these two locks in other words about 30 minutes per lock. Henry, Illinois is at Mile 196. The trip is quite scenic passing through farmland and small towns. We stayed at the Henry Harbor Marina which had a motel and restaurant.

Henry Harbor Marina Phone: (309) 364-2181

Accepts Transients	yes	**Mechanical Repairs**	no
Dockside Power	30	**Ships Store**	no
Dockside Water	yes	**Showers**	yes
Gasoline	yes	**Laundromat**	no
Diesel Fuel	yes	**Restaurant**	yes

Henry, Illinois to Browning, Illinois

The trip from Henry to Browning is 99 miles and includes 1 lock at Peoria (Mile 147.7). Peoria is known for the Par-A-Dice which is a 228-ft. long stern-wheeler riverboat casino. We passed the Par-A-Dice, which was underway when we went through Peoria. We had another interesting experience in the Peoria Lock. When we got to the lock, a tow was waiting to go in. Since this tow was only going to use half of the lock, we called the Lockmaster on the radio and asked if we could lock through with the tow. The Lockmaster, in this case, must ask the tow captain for his permission and he said yes, so we moved into the lock after the tow was already in. Our normal practice when in a lock is to hold our boat to the side of the lock by looping the lock lines under a cleat and then playing out the line as our boat descends. We learned that when in a lock with a tow you must tie the lock line tight to the cleat as soon as the boat reaches the lower water level. The reason for this is that when the tow starts its powerful engines, the backwash against the rear gate causes severe turbulence, which blew our boat away from the wall because we were not tied tight to our cleats.

Browning, Illinois is a small town of approximately 200 including cats and dogs. The main industry believe it or not is fishing. These people fish the Illinois River for buffalo, carp and catfish with nets using 24 feet long by 8 feet wide-open boats. We talked to one fisherman that we met at the restaurant at the River's Edge Boat Club. He told us that he and his partner catch 10 tons of fish per week. They go out each morning until their open boat is filled with fish. They then pull their boat filled with fish onto a trailer and haul it to a wholesale fish dealer. Most of this type of fish is used for cat food, etc. The River's Edge Boat Club is a restaurant on pilings at the river's edge with a barge containing gas and diesel pumps. We tied up to the gas barge for the night. The restaurant had a $5.00, all you can eat, fish dinner featuring the local fish. The catfish was ok, but we didn't like the buffalo or the carp.

River's Edge Boat Club Phone: (217) 323-4780

Accepts Transients	yes	**Mechanical Repairs**	no
Dockside Power	no	**Ships Store**	no
Dockside Water	no	**Showers**	no
Gasoline	yes	**Laundromat**	no
Diesel Fuel	yes	**Restaurant**	yes

Browning, Illinois to Portage de Sioux, Missouri

The trip from Browning, Illinois to the Mississippi is 97.5 miles with 1 lock, the La Grange Lock, at Mile Marker 80.2. The scenery is farmland and beautiful countryside. The last

6 miles of today's trip is on the Mississippi. We stayed at "My River Home Harbor" Marina at the town of Portage de Sioux on the Missouri side of the river. Portage de Sioux is at Mississippi River Mile Marker 212.4 and is 32 miles north of downtown St. Louis. There are several marinas in this area, but there are no marinas and no docks in St. Louis. You either stay 32 miles north or 22 miles south of St. Louis at Hoppies Marina in Kimmswick, Missouri.

My River Home Harbor Phone: (314) 899-0903

Accepts Transients	yes	**Mechanical Repairs**	yes
Dockside Power	30	**Ships Store**	yes
Dockside Water	yes	**Showers**	yes
Gasoline	yes	**Laundromat**	yes
Diesel Fuel	yes	**Restaurant**	yes

St. Louis, Missouri

If you wish to go sight seeing in St. Louis, you will need to rent a car to get from the marina to downtown St. Louis. The Gateway Arch is the most famous monument on the Mississippi and at 630 feet tall is the tallest in the U.S. A tram system carries visitors to the observation room at the top. There is a museum and theater at the bottom. St. Louis has some excellent museums and a famous botanical garden and zoo. St. Louis also has many good restaurants and riverboat gambling.

The Mississippi River

The Mississippi River is divided into two parts, namely the Upper Mississippi and the Lower Mississippi. The Upper Mississippi starts in Minneapolis and runs 858 miles long to

Cairo, Illinois, which is where the Ohio River joins the Mississippi. The Upper Mississippi is more scenic than the Lower and has marinas to service recreational boating. The Lower Mississippi goes from Cairo, Illinois to New Orleans, Louisiana, which is a total of 856 miles. The Lower Mississippi has few harbors and long distances between gas stops. The barge traffic is very heavy and there is very little recreational boating. The current in the Mississippi can be 6 mph in the spring and average 2 to 4 mph normally. The Mississippi is also known for floating debris, which can be as large as a telephone pole. For all of these reasons, I recommend that you leave the Mississippi at Cairo, Illinois and take the alternative Tenn-Tom route to the Gulf. If you take the Tenn-Tom route, you will be on the Mississippi for 218 miles from where the Illinois River joins the Mississippi to Cairo, Illinois, which is Upper Mississippi Mile 1.

Portage de Sioux to Ste. Genevieve, Missouri

The trip from Portage de Sioux to Ste. Genevieve, Missouri is 90 miles and there are two locks. We had a 3-mph current in our favor so we made good time. Portage de Sioux is at Upper Mississippi Mile 212 with the two locks being at Mile 200.8 and 185.0. As a point of reference, the famous St. Louis Gateway Arch is at Mile Marker 180. The Gateway Arch is especially impressive from the water. The tows on the Illinois River were large; however, the tows on the Mississippi are even larger. We saw many tows that were three barges wide and several which were four barges wide. All the barges seem to be a standard size of 25 feet wide by 50 feet long. I am told that each barge holds the equivalent of 50 eighteen wheeler trucks. Therefore, a tow with 3 barges wide by 5 long would carry as much material as 750 trucks.

Marina de Gabouri in Ste. Genevieve, Missouri is in a little cove so it is out of the Mississippi current. The marina is basically a gas dock, which on the day we were there had four boats all in the 30 to 40 ft. size that used up all the dock space. On the entire trip we never met another boat that was on the Great Circle Cruise except on this day. All three of the other boats at this marina were on the Great Circle Cruise and were travelling together. These boats had started in Florida in April 1996 and would finish in November seven months later. We would see these boats again at our Anchorage at Cairo, Illinois and at our next marina, which would be on the Cumberland River.

Staying at this particular marina is very important since it is the last gas for 175 miles and the last marina for 204 miles. This created a special problem for us because we only have a range of 120 miles when cruising at 18 mph. Boats with diesel engines have much longer ranges and this would not be a problem. To handle this problem, our plan was to run at 10 mph for the 121 miles to Cairo, Illinois to conserve fuel. Since we had a 3-mph current in our favor, we would actually make 13-mph speed over ground. At Cairo, Illinois, we would anchor out for the night and add 50 gallons of gas from 10 five-gallon gas cans that we carried on our aft deck. The next day we would cruise up the Ohio River 53 miles to the gas dock. Even though we would be bucking the current on the Ohio River, we calculated that 50 gallons extra should be enough.

Marina de Gabouri Phone: (314) 883-5599

Accepts Transients	yes	**Mechanical Repairs**	no
Dockside Power	30,50	**Ships Store**	yes
Dockside Water	yes	**Showers**	yes

Gasoline	yes	**Laundromat**	no
Diesel Fuel	yes	**Restaurant**	yes

Ste. Genevieve, Missouri to Cairo, Illinois

About a month before flying back to Chicago to resume the trip, I ordered the 10 five-gallon gas cans from Boat/US and had them shipped to Marina de Gabouri. The marina held them for me until our arrival so we didn't have to store them on the boat. When we arrived at the marina, the gas pump was broken and they were working on it to fix it. Unfortunately, they didn't get the gas pump fixed until 10 a.m. the next morning. By the time we filled our gas tanks with 240 gallons and filled the 10 gas cans with another 50 gallons, it was 11:00 a.m. In retrospect, we should have waited until the next morning to leave, but we didn't. Since we were travelling at the slow speed of 10 mph through the water, it got dark before we arrived at our Anchorage at Cairo, Illinois. We had a built-in search light on the boat that could be moved with four buttons. This turned out to be almost worthless in trying to spot markers on the very dark Mississippi River. What we should have had was a hand held halogen light that operates from the cigarette lighter at the helm with a 12-ft. flexible cord. The next time we were caught running in the dark, we had the halogen light, which worked great to find the channel. We arrived at our Anchorage after running in the dark and guessing where the channel was for the last hour.

The Anchorage was in a cove, which was out of the Mississippi current on the Illinois side and the north side of the bridge that crosses the Mississippi at Cairo, Illinois. The three boats that were also on the Great Circle Cruise were diesel and, therefore, were unaffected by the gas pump problem. When we arrived at the Anchorage, the three boats were already anchored there. We anchored out for the night, and the next morning we put 25 gallons into each of our two tanks.

Cairo, Illinois to Grand Rivers, Kentucky

We had 53 miles to go on the Ohio River to get gas. The gas dock is at Ohio Mile 928.4, and the Tennessee River is at Ohio Mile 934.2. The Ohio River starts with Mile 1 in Pittsburgh, Pennsylvania and ends at Cairo, Illinois, which is Ohio Mile 981. What this means is that we had to go 6 miles past the Tennessee River to get gas and then come back those 6 miles to the Tennessee River. Since we were bucking the current on the Ohio, we covered only about 15 miles when cruising at 18 mph through the water. There were two locks on the Ohio River; one at Ohio Mile 962.6, and the second at Mile 938.9. When we got to the gas dock, we filled both tanks, and I calculated that if we had not carried the extra 50 gallons, we would have been 16 gallons short of making the gas dock. I gave the empty gas cans to the lady at the gas dock and she was very appreciative. I did not want to carry 10 used empty gas cans on the boat.

We left the gas dock and went 6 miles to be Tennessee River and then 21 miles up the Tennessee River to the Kentucky Dam. The Kentucky Dam Lock was a lift of 57 ft. and uses floating bollards to tie your boat to in the lock. The floating bollard makes it much easier to hold your boat to the side of the lock using only one line between a mid-cleat on your boat and the bollard. We were very lucky in that just as we got to the Kentucky Dam Lock they were taking pleasure boats into the lock. We found out that some of those boats had been waiting for four hours. Commercial traffic has the right-of-way at these locks, and if there is commercial traffic, the pleasure boats have to wait. When you come through the lock there is a large marina on the Tennessee River; however, the Green Turtle Marina, two miles away on the Cumberland River, had been recommended to us so we went there. It turned out to be a good choice. They had a Yacht Club there which transients could go to for dinner. We stayed there several days to relax.

Green Turtle Marina Phone: (502) 362-8364

Accepts Transients	yes	**Mechanical Repairs**	yes
Dockside Power	30,50	**Ships Store**	yes
Dockside Water	yes	**Showers**	yes
Gasoline	yes	**Laundromat**	yes
Diesel Fuel	yes	**Restaurant**	yes

Grand Rivers, Kentucky to Waverly, Tennessee

The Tennessee River is a beautiful river, especially the part that we travel on this trip, which is known as the Kentucky Lake. The Kentucky Lake is that part of the Tennessee River between the Kentucky Dam and the Pickwick Dam and is 180 miles long. This long lake has five state parks and 80 resorts on its shores. At its northern end is the area known as *"The Land Between The Lakes"*, which is a very large resort area run by the Tennessee Valley Authority. Our trip to Waverly, Tennessee and the Cuba Landing Marina is 92 miles long and is all beautiful lake. We only saw about one tow per hour as compared to the Mississippi with one tow every 10 minutes. The Cuba Landing Marina had just been rebuilt with new docks, ships store, etc. in 1996. They lent us a courtesy van and Charlie and I went to a restaurant and had chicken fried steak.

Cuba Landing Marina Phone: (615) 296-2822

Accepts Transients	yes	Mechanical Repairs	yes
Dockside Power	30,50	Ships Store	yes
Dockside Water	yes	Showers	yes
Gasoline	yes	Laundromat	yes
Diesel Fuel	yes	Restaurant	no

Waverly, Tennessee to Iuka, Mississippi

The trip to Iuka, Mississippi is 104 miles with the first 91 miles on the Kentucky Lake to the Pickwick Dam and Lock. The Pickwick Lock has a lift of 55 feet and is at Tennessee Mile 206.7. After going through the lock, you continue on the Tennessee River for about 8 miles to the junction with the Tenn-Tom Waterway (Tennessee Mile 215 and Tenn-Tom Mile 452). Following the Tenn-Tom, the Aqua Yacht Harbor is only 4 miles away. The Aqua Yacht Harbor is quite large including swimming pool, tennis court, restaurant and courtesy vans. Charlie Frame got a ride to Memphis and flew home to Philadelphia on Thursday. My wife, Jeri, and our friends, George and Anaruth Hynson, were not scheduled to arrive from Memphis until Sunday so I had three days alone where I didn't have to move the boat, which was relaxing. I borrowed the courtesy car and visited the Shiloh Battlefield Park on one day, which I would recommend.

Aqua Yacht Harbor Phone: (601) 423-2222

Accepts Transients	yes	Mechanical Repairs	yes
Dockside Power	30,50	Ships Store	yes
Dockside Water	yes	Showers	yes
Gasoline	yes	Laundromat	yes
Diesel Fuel	yes	Restaurant	yes

A tow pushing into a lock on the Illinois River

Nittany Navy docked on the Illinois River

Approaching St. Louis in The Mississippi

The Mississippi Queen

Tenn-Tom Canal to Mobile, Alabama Tenn-Tom Waterway System

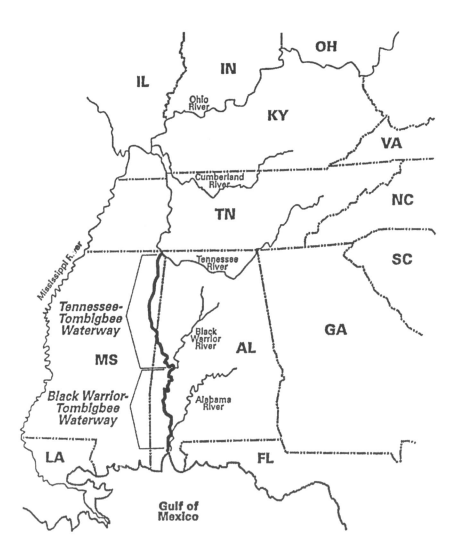

Destination	Distance (Statute Miles) Between Points		Cumulative
Iuka, MS	0		0
Smithville, MS	72	(4 locks)	72
Carrolton, AL	69	(4 locks)	141
Demopolis, AL	91	(2 locks)	232
Bashi Creek, AL (Anchorage)	72	(1 lock)	304
Lady's Landing, AL	65	(1 lock)	369
Mobile, AL	87		456

Charts Required:

U.S. Army Corps of Engineers Charts
  Charts of the Tennessee-Tombigbee Waterway
  Lower Block Warrior-Tombigbee Waterway Charts

Waterway Guide: *Quimby's Cruising Guide*

NOTE: The destinations where the author stayed are shown in bold type and are described in the following chapter. The other destinations are listed as intermediate ports if a shorter cruising day is desired. Check the waterway guide for information on intermediate ports.

The Tenn-Tom Waterway

The Tenn-Tom Waterway connects the Tennessee River in Mississippi to the Black Warrior River in Alabama. This Waterway system provides a parallel route to the lower Mississippi when traveling from the upper Mississippi to the Gulf. The Waterway system is 450 miles long and has 12 locks. The system lowers your boat from an elevation of 341 feet at the Tennessee River to sea level at Mobile, Alabama.

As previously stated, this is a much more pristine and relaxing way to cruise to the Gulf than taking the lower Mississippi.

The canal project was started in 1972 and finished in 1985. It was the largest project ever undertaken by the Army Corps of Engineers costing 2 billion dollars. The amount of dirt that was moved was greater than for the Panama Canal. The 12 locks are all 600 feet long by 110 feet wide and are of the latest design using floating bollards to tie up to when in the lock. The floating bollards are built into the sides of the lock and float up and down with the water level. You only need to tie one line from a center cleat on your boat to the floating bollard to hold you boat to the side of the lock. The Tenn-Tom Waterway has more recreational boats than commercial boats and is the main route in spring and fall for recreational boats travelling between the Mid-West and Florida.

During our trip down the Tenn-Tom, we passed hundreds of bass boats and quite a few duck hunters in their camouflaged boats. The duck hunters on the Tenn-Tom are famous for shooting their guns over top of boats that throw a wake on them. Since the duck hunters are hiding from the ducks, they are often in the shade on the side of the Waterway and are very hard to see. Therefore, it can easily happen that you inadvertently throw a wake on them. The Waterway system travels through extremely rural sections of Mississippi and Alabama.

Iuka, Mississippi to Smithville, Mississippi

Our first day on the Tenn-Tom we went 72 miles and passed through 4 locks. The Tenn-Tom was prettier than expected with very little barge or boat traffic at all. Since it was late

September, many of the boats we saw were going in our direction and were headed for Florida. At the third lock "Lock D", a 55 foot Viking pulled out of the lock in front of us out of turn. We followed in their wake at 18 knots until we came to the Midway Marina and slowed down, however, the Viking did not slow down. When we got to the fourth lock "Lock C", the police were waiting for the Viking. When the lock opened, we followed the Viking into the lock and tied up to a floating bollard. The police came over to the Viking and asked the captain to get off the boat. They arrested the captain and took him away in a police car. We talked to the police before we left the lock and they said that the Viking had caused possibly $2,000 worth of damage at the Midway Marina.

We followed the Viking, with someone else piloting, to the Smithville Marina. Several hours later, the captain of the Viking arrived at the Marina. He had had a hearing before a Justice Of The Peace and had had to post an $800 bond to assure his appearance in their Court at a later date. The people at the Marina told us that the Midway Marina was famous for having people arrested who didn't slow down when going past their Marina. We borrowed the marinas courtesy car and went into Smithville to buy food to eat on our boat. The only food available was catfish, barbecue, ribs and chicken. The food was good, however we found out that for the next four nights the only food available from local restaurants were the same four things. After several nights we had had enough of the local cuisine and we switched to food we had on board.

Smithville Marina Phone: (205) 373-6701

Approach Depth	10'	**Diesel Fuel**	yes
Dockside Depth	7'	**Mechanical Repairs**	no

Accepts Transients	yes	Ships Store	no
Dockside Power	30,50	Showers	yes
Dockside Water	yes	Laundromat	yes
Gasoline	yes	Restaurant	no

Smithville, Mississippi to Carrolton, Alabama

The second day on the Tenn-Tom we went 69 miles and did 4 locks. The scenery continued to be beautiful, and because of the dams, the water is very tranquil. We stayed at the Marina Cove Marina in Carrolton, Alabama. The Marina is located only one mile from the Tom Bevell lock and museum. The Museum is a beautiful reproduction of a southern mansion and is a shrine to Tom Bevell, who as an Alabama Congressman, was chairman of the Waterways Subcommittee who got the money to build the Tenn-Tom Waterway. The Museum is quite interesting and documents the building of the Waterway.

The restaurants in Carrolton are open only Thursday, Friday and Saturday. We were there on a Tuesday so we bought barbecue and took it to the boat. The entire region through which the Waterway runs seems to be "dry" counties in Mississippi and Alabama. If you like to have beer or wine with dinner, be sure to bring it with you before you start the Tenn-Tom.

Marina Cove Marina Phone: (205) 373-6701

Approach Depth	9'	Diesel Fuel	yes
Dockside Depth	7'	Mechanical Repairs	no
Accepts Transients	yes	Ships Store	no
Dockside Power	30,50	Showers	yes
Dockside Water	yes	Laundromat	yes
Gasoline	yes	Restaurant	no

Carrolton, Alabama to Demopolis, Alabama

The third day on the Tenn-Tom we went 91 miles and passed through 2 locks. We continued to be amazed by the small amount of boat traffic, both pleasure and commercial. The tows are small compared to the Mississippi River. The typical tows on the Tenn-Tom were only 2 to 6 barges per tow. Demopolis is at the mouth of the Black Warrior River, which is approximately the halfway point on the Waterway and where you change chart books. The Demopolis Yacht Basin is the Marina where we stayed. The Marina was large for the Tenn-Tom and had a restaurant and bar. The tows stop at the Demopolis Yacht Basin to refuel, which takes some hours since the tows can carry several thousand gallons of diesel fuel.

Demopolis Yacht Basin Phone: (334) 289-4647

Approach Depth	18'	**Diesel Fuel**	yes
Dockside Depth	18'	**Mechanical Repairs**	yes
Accepts Transients	yes	**Ships Store**	yes
Dockside Power	30,50	**Showers**	yes
Dockside Water	yes	**Laundromat**	yes
Gasoline	yes	**Restaurant**	yes

Demopolis, Alabama to Lady's Landing, Alabama

The trip from Demopolis to Lady's Landing is 137 miles with 2 locks. This can be done in one or two days with an anchorage since there are no marinas between these two points. If you wish to make the trip in two days, you can anchor out at Bashi Creek, which is 72 miles from Demopolis. Alternately, if you choose to do the 137 miles in one day as we did, you can get gas at Bobby's fish camp, which is 98 miles from Demopolis. Bobby's fish camp does not have any overnight docking.

Lady's Landing is a floating dock at the bottom of a steep bank about 20 feet high. The gas and diesel pumps are at the top of the bank and hoses run down the bank to the floating dock. To go from the floating dock to the top of the bank there is a wooden staircase with a landing at the top. There is a rather large goat on the landing that you must pet in order to get by. The goat's name is Billy, and when you scratch his head, he moves over to let you pass. We asked the people at the Marina if there was a restaurant nearby and they said the closest restaurant was in a town 10 miles away and for $20 they would drive us there, wait for us to have dinner, and then drive us home. I asked what type of restaurant it was and was told it was a "Hardee's". We had a nice dinner on our boat.

Lady's Landing Phone: (205) 246-2903

Approach Depth	10'	**Diesel Fuel**	yes
Dockside Depth	6'	**Mechanical Repairs**	no
Accepts Transients	yes	**Ships Store**	no
Dockside Power	30	**Showers**	no
Dockside Water	yes	**Laundromat**	no
Gasoline	yes	**Restaurant**	no

Lady's Landing, Alabama to Mobile, Alabama

We left Lady's Landing at 8:00 a.m. with some light fog above the water. The fog burnt off and we had another sunny day to finish the Tenn-Tom. About an hour out of Lady's Landing we heard a rifle shot and we looked back to see a duck hunter standing in his camouflaged boat and waving his gun at us.

We had gone 5 days on the Tenn-Tom without being "shot over" because we were very careful to look for the hunters and slow down, however, we didn't see this boat. It is 80 miles from Lady's Landing to downtown Mobile, plus another 7 miles to Dog River where all the marinas are. The last 20 miles before Mobile, the river gradually widens into Mobile Bay. Downtown Mobile is quite impressive with new, modern buildings and a busy port.

Mobile, Alabama

We stayed at the Grand Mariner Marina, which had a good seafood restaurant on the premises. One of their specialties was big red shrimp steamed in Old Bay Seasoning. You peel the shrimp and dip them in butter. They were so good, I had them twice as a dinner. We rented a car from Enterprise since we were about 8 miles from downtown Mobile. The second day in Mobile it rained all day, and so we stayed on the boat and watched Penn State beat Wisconsin in a "squeaker". The next day we took George and Anaruth Hynson to the airport in the morning. That night, Jeri and I had dinner at NanSeas, a very nice waterfront restaurant close to the marina. The next day, we picked up our next crew at the Mobile Airport our son, Scott, and his wife, Bonnie. They would go with us to New Orleans.

Grand Mariner Marina Phone: (334) 443-6300

Approach Depth	15'	**Diesel Fuel**	yes
Dockside Depth	15'	**Mechanical Repairs**	yes
Accepts Transients	yes	**Ships Store**	yes
Dockside Power	30,50	**Showers**	yes
Dockside Water	yes	**Laundromat**	yes
Gasoline	yes	**Restaurant**	yes

The proper way to tie from a mid-cleat to a floating bollard in a Tenn-Tom Lock

Fisherman in the Tenn-Tom

White Cliffs on the Tenn-Tom

The goat at Lady's Landing

Dinner on Board, Jeri with George and Anaruth Hynson

Mobile, Alabama waterfront

*Mobile to New Orleans
to Carrabelle, Florida
Gulf Intracoastal Waterway*

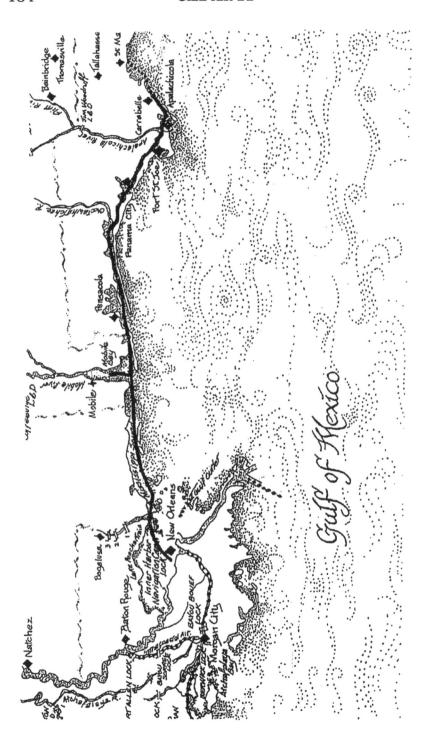

Destination	Distance (Statute Miles) Between Points	Cumulative
Mobile, AL	0	0
Biloxi, MS	85	85
Bay St. Louis, MS	66	151
New Orleans, LA	40	191
Biloxi, MS	106	297
Pensacola, FL	97	394
Destin, FL	30	424
Panama City, FL	45	469
Carrabelle, FL	80	549

Charts Required:
BBA Chart Kit – New Orleans to Panama City, Florida
BBA Chart Kit – Florida's West Coast and the Keys

Waterway Guide:
Waterway Guide - Southern

NOTE: The destinations where the author stayed are shown in bold type and are described in the following chapter. The other destinations are listed as intermediate ports if a shorter cruising day is desired. Check the waterway guide for information on intermediate ports.

The Gulf Intracoastal Waterway (GIWW)

The Gulf Intracoastal Waterway runs 1,000 miles from Carrabelle, Florida to Brownsville, Texas. Distances on the Gulf Intracoastal are measured in statute miles east or west of Harvey Lock in New Orleans and shown as EHL or WHL. On our trip we entered the Gulf Intracoastal at the Mobile Bay Ship Channel, which was GIWW mile 134 EHL. We left the GIWW at 34 EHL to go to Lake Pontchartrain and New Orleans. When returning, we reentered the Gulf Intracoastal at 34 EHL and took it all the way to Carrabelle, which is 380 EHL. The Gulf Intracoastal Waterway runs between a series of barrier islands and the mainland similar to the East Coast Intracoastal Waterway. The channel is dredged to 10 feet and is well marked.

Mobile, Alabama to Biloxi, Mississippi

The trip from Mobile to Biloxi is 85 miles long with the first 20 miles in Mobile Bay. We ran in the rain and had a beam sea in Mobile Bay, which became a following sea when we turned west into the Gulf Intracoastal Waterway. The sea was fairly rough and for only the second time on the entire trip, we had a crewmember that was seasick. We left Mobile at 8:30 a.m. and arrived at Biloxi at 1 p.m., 4.5 hours later. The rain stopped and the sun came out as we arrived in Biloxi. We stayed at the Point Cadet Marina, which is right next to three casinos.

Biloxi, Mississippi

Biloxi, Mississippi is a casino town with at least 8 casinos and more being built. The Mississippi casino law stretches the riverboat casino law to the limit. The casino hotels in Biloxi have the hotel part built on land and the casino part built on a barge chained to the dock. The casino is floating, but there is no way it could move. All the casinos have a number of restaurants plus entertainment, so this turned out to be an interesting place to dock. One of the casinos next to the marina is "Casino Magic", which had a free comedy show the night we were there that was terrific.

Point Cadet Marina Phone: (601) 436-9312

Approach Depth	12'	Diesel Fuel	no
Dockside Depth	10'	Mechanical Repairs	no
Accepts Transients	yes	Ships Store	yes
Dockside Power	30,50,100	Showers	yes
Dockside Water	yes	Laundromat	yes
Gasoline	no	Restaurant	at casino

Biloxi, Mississippi to New Orleans, Louisiana

The distance from Biloxi to New Orleans is 106 miles where the first 71 miles is on the Gulf Intracoastal Waterway. You leave the GIWW at mile 34 EHL, entering the Rigolets through the L & N Railroad swing bridge. The Rigolets is a canal that joins Lake Borgne and Lake Pontchartrain. When staying in New Orleans, all the marinas are on Lake Pontchartrain not on the Mississippi River. Once in Lake Pontchartrain, you go about 25 miles across the lake to get to the marina area. The marina area is on the south shore of the lake and about two miles east of the causeway that crosses the lake. Since we were planning to spend five days in New Orleans, we rented a car because the distance from the marina area to the French Quarter is about eight miles. We stayed at the Orleans Marina, which was large and had all the amenities.

Orleans Marina Phone: (504) 288-2351

Approach Depth	9'	Diesel Fuel	no
Dockside Depth	12'	Mechanical Repairs	no
Accepts Transients	yes	Ships Store	yes
Dockside Power	30,50,100	Showers	yes
Dockside Water	yes	Laundromat	yes
Gasoline	no	Restaurant	nearby

New Orleans, Louisiana

The trip to New Orleans added 340 miles to the overall trip, but I think it was well worth it if you haven't been there. The distance from the end of Mobile Bay to New Orleans is 170 miles, and since you have to come back to Mobile Bay to continue east on the main trip, the side trip to New Orleans becomes 340 miles total. I had been to New Orleans several times on business, however, my wife Jeri, son Scott, and daughter-in-law Bonnie, had never been there before. New Orleans is a unique place that blends French and American culture as in no other place.

Our first night in New Orleans, we had dinner at "Joe's Crab", which was walking distance from the marina. This restaurant was the only restaurant I have ever been in that offered all five kinds of crab; Blue, Dungeness, Snow, Stone and Softshell. The next day we went to the French Quarter, took the trolley tour of the city, had dinner at Antoines after which we did Bourbon Street. The next day, we had breakfast at Brennans, which is quite an experience. This is not a buffet but is a three course, fixed price breakfast where you can select from 5 or 6 choices for each course. Their signature desert is "Banana's Foster", which they invented. During the next several days, we took a ride on the "Delta Queen", which is a full size Mississippi Paddlewheel boat, took a plantation tour, and had some other fine meals.

New Orleans was the end of the second leg of our trip so we planned to leave our boat there for 3.5 months. Normally, when we leave our boat for some months, we have it pulled out of the water and stored on land, which is cheaper. However, there was no dry storage possible in New Orleans. I made a deal with the Orleans Marina to leave my boat in its slip for 30 cents per foot instead of 1 dollar per foot with the condition that I get my boat out of there before the Super Bowl. We flew home from New Orleans on October 7, 1996, and returned on January 17, 1997, to resume the trip.

New Orleans, Louisiana to Biloxi, Mississippi

We arrived back in New Orleans at 1 p.m. on January 17 to continue our journey. The next day, we left at 9:30 a.m. headed for Biloxi. We arrived at Biloxi at 2:00 p.m., however, coming into Biloxi, I got confused as to where the channel was and we ran aground. The props were touching bottom, but the boat was floating. We were able to slowly back out while churning sand. A man in a small boat showed us the way to the channel. Once in the channel when we speeded up, there was severe vibration. The boat ran without vibration below 1,000 rpm. We went back to the Point Cadet Marina where we had stayed last fall. At the marina, we had a diver check our props. He was unable to remove them, however, he couldn't see any damage which led us to believe we had bent shafts.

We had arrived in Biloxi on a Saturday, so we would have to wait until Monday to get into a shipyard to pull the boat out of the water. At the Point Cadet Marina the boat that was docked next to us was owned by a man named Les Lala. He told us about Cavacevich Boatyard and he showed up at 8 a.m. on Monday morning to call them to see if they could work on our boat immediately. They said they could take the boat, so we slowly cruised over to the boatyard at 1,000 rpm, which took an hour. Les drove over to the boatyard to see that we were taken care of. He even offered to let us stay in his house while the boat was being repaired; what a guy! The boat was pulled out of the water and it was found that both shafts were bent and both props were also. We rented an Enterprise car and checked into the Casino Grand Hotel (which Les also arranged).

The lesson that I learned here was that when I first became confused as to where we were, I should have stopped and taken a fix. Secondly I learned that in the future if I ran aground, I should immediately shut the engines off and call for a tow, not try to plow my way out. The Cavacevich Boatyard did a fantastic job in straightening both shafts and props and having our boat ready to go by 12:30 the next day. The bill I thought was reasonable and our boat insurance picked up all but $300.

Biloxi, Mississippi to Pensacola, Florida

The trip from Biloxi to Pensacola is 97 miles on the Gulf Intracoastal, however, since we got such a late start at 12:30 p.m., we would not make it to Pensacola that day. By 5:30 p.m. it was starting to get dark and we came upon a 50 foot motor yacht doing 10 knots in our direction. We talked on the radio and found that they were going to the Bear Point Marina, which was 30 miles west of Pensacola. We followed them to the marina, gassed up, had dinner on board, and went to bed early. The next day we decided to skip Pensacola and go right to Destin where we were meeting our next crew and where we were also visiting friends. However, the data for the marina we had planned to stay at in Pensacola is as follows.

Harbor Village at Pitt Slip Marina Phone: (904) 432-9620

Approach Depth	10'	**Diesel Fuel**	yes
Dockside Depth	9'	**Mechanical Repairs**	yes

Accepts Transients	yes	**Ships Store**	yes
Dockside Power	30,50	**Showers**	yes
Dockside Water	yes	**Laundromat**	yes
Gasoline	yes	**Restaurant**	nearby

Pensacola, Florida to Destin, Florida

The distance from Pensacola to Destin is only 30 miles, however, Destin is a very popular beach resort and a nice place to visit. We pulled into Sandestin's Baytowne Marina and called our friends Guy and Thea Woodluff who owned a condo in Destin. We would spend the next several days with them and be joined by our next crew who were Peter and Maria Doelp. I played golf with Guy in Destin, which was the only time I played golf on the entire boat trip. This tells you how much fun the boat trip was since I normally play golf twice a week.

Sandestin's Baytowne Marina Phone: (904) 267-7777

Approach Depth	7.5'	**Diesel Fuel**	yes
Dockside Depth	6'	**Mechanical Repairs**	yes
Accepts Transients	yes	**Ships Store**	yes
Dockside Power	30,50,100	**Showers**	yes
Dockside Water	yes	**Laundromat**	yes
Gasoline	yes	**Restaurant**	yes

Destin, Florida to Panama City, Florida

The distance between Destin and Panama City is only 45 miles. There was a storm forecast for the afternoon so we ran ahead of the storm and got there before 1:00 p.m. We watched the storm from a restaurant next to the Bay Point Marina. The Bay Point Marina is actually in Panama City Beach, which is on a Barrier Island on the other side of the

Intracoastal Waterway from Panama City. However, you might consider staying in Panama City, which has many marinas and is the largest Marine Center on the Florida Coast north of Tampa.

Bay Point Marina Phone: (904) 235-6911

Approach Depth	6'	Diesel Fuel	yes
Dockside Depth	6'	Mechanical Repairs	yes
Accepts Transients	yes	Ships Store	yes
Dockside Power	30,50,100	Showers	yes
Dockside Water	yes	Laundromat	yes
Gasoline	yes	Restaurant	yes

Panama City to Carrabelle, Florida

We had nice weather for the 80 mile trip from Panama City to Carrabelle. Cruising the Gulf Intracoastal Waterway is quite scenic and the channels are well marked. Carrabelle is at the eastern end of the Gulf Intracoastal Waterway and is a favorite jumping off place to cross the Gulf to the West Coast of Florida.

Carrabelle, Florida

Since the trip from Carrabelle to Cedar Keys is 120 miles straight across the Gulf and 180 miles to Tarpon Springs, it is prudent to wait for good weather before crossing. I have talked to people who had to wait as long as two weeks in Carrabelle before the weather was good enough for the crossing. The town is well equipped to service yachtsmen waiting to make the crossing. Carrabelle was a place where we made another crew change with Peter and Maria Doelp leaving and George and Helen Roth arriving. We were staying at the Moorings Marina and we made arrangements through them for a driver to take the Doelps to the Tallahassee Airport and bring the Roths back. The crew switch was made on Super Bowl Sunday 1997. We ate on the boat that night and watched Green Bay win the Super Bowl.

The Morrings Marina Phone: (904) 697-2800

Approach Depth	15'	**Diesel Fuel**	yes
Dockside Depth	10'	**Mechanical Repairs**	yes
Accepts Transients	yes	**Ships Store**	yes
Dockside Power	30,50	**Showers**	yes
Dockside Water	yes	**Laundromat**	yes
Gasoline	yes	**Restaurant**	nearby

New Orleans

Street musicians in New Orleans

Crew No. 7 at New Orleans; Scott, Bonnie, Jeri and Bick Remmey

Props and shafts being straightened in Biloxi, Mississippi

Carrabelle, Florida to Key West
West Coast of Florida

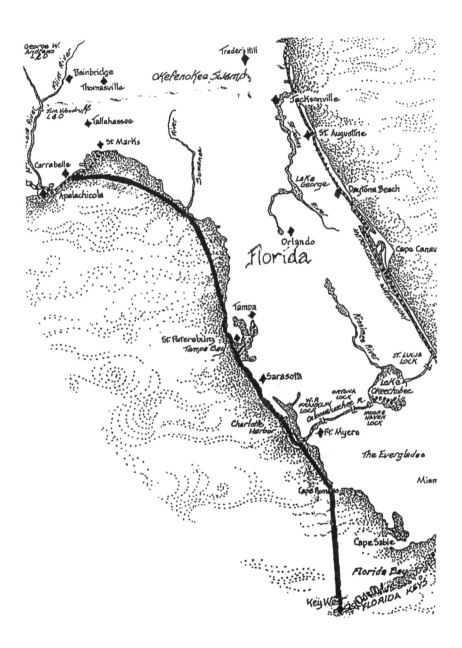

George W. Andrews L&D

Bainbridge

Flint River

Thomasville

Jim Woodruff L&D

Tallahassee

Carrabelle

Apalachicola

St Marks

Suwanee River

Trader's Hill

Okefenokea Swamp

Jacksonville

St. Johns River

St. Augustine

Lake George

Daytona Beach

Orlando

Florida

Cape Canav.

Intracoastal Waterway

Tampa

St Petersburg

Tampa Bay

Sarasota

Kissimee River

ST. LUCIE LOCK

Lake Okeechobee

ORTONA LOCK

W.P. FRANKLIN LOCK

Caloosahatchee R.

MOORE HAVEN LOCK

Charlotte Harbor

Ft. Myers

The Everglades

Miam

Cape Romano

Cape Sable

Florida Bay

Key West

FLORIDA KEYS

Destination	Distance (Statute Miles) Between Points	Cumulative
Carrabelle, FL	0	0
Cedar Key, FL	125	125
Tarpon, Springs, FL	60	185
St. Petersburg, FL	45	230
Longboat Key, FL	20	250
Boca Grande, FL	43	293
Marco Island, FL	65	358
Key West, FL	98	456

Charts Required:
BBA Chart Kit – Florida's West Coast and The Keys

Waterway Guide:
Waterway Guide - Southern

NOTE: The destinations where the author stayed are shown in bold type and are described in the following chapter. The other destinations are listed as intermediate ports if a shorter cruising day is desired. Check the waterway guide for information on intermediate ports.

Carrabelle to Cedar Keys

The trip from Carrabelle to Cedar Keys is 120 miles and from Cedar Keys to Tarpon Springs is 50 miles. There is no gas or diesel at Cedar Keys, so you must have a range of 180 miles since you can't fill up until Tarpon Springs. Our boat had a range of only 120 miles, so we went to Suwannee River which is only 105 miles from Carrabelle and has gas and diesel. However, you can only get into Suwannee River at high tide. We were lucky that we arrived at high tide. If I had it to do over again in the same boat, I would have carried an extra 100 gallons of gas aboard in plastic Jerry cans and skipped Suwannee River.

We expected to leave Carrabelle at 8:00 a.m., however, the weather forecast was too windy to go straight across and the weather was supposed to get worse later in the week. The people at the Moorings Marina showed me a protected route which stayed within 10 miles of shore all the way across and therefore shielded us from the East winds. We finally left at 10:00 a.m. and the route turned out to be great. It was mildly rough for the first two hours after which it got quite smooth. The protected route from Carrabelle to Cedar Keys is as follows:

Protected Route
Carrabelle to Cedar Key

Chart Book

Page 2		From Carrabelle follow channel to R "12" at southern end of Dog Island. Continue in Channel to R "2" (29° 44.5'/84° 39.2')
	C079	16.5 nm to R "20" at (29° 47.9'/84° 20.7')
Page 22	C070	9.8 nm to R "24" (29° 51.5'/84° 10.3')
	C084	15.7 nm to R "22" (29° 53.4'/83° 53.3')
Page 21	C121	9.8 nm to R "20" (29° 48.5'/83° 43.3')

	C142	10.9 nm to R "18" (29° 40.1'/83° 35.3')
Page 20	C154	13.1 nm to R "16" (29° 28.5'/83° 28.4')
Page 19	C152	10.2 nm to R "14" (29° 19.6'/83° 22.6')
	C119	10.7 nm to R "2" (29° 14.6'/83° 11.8')
	C153	7.1 nm to 16 ft. R "2" (29° 08.4'/83° 07.9')
Page 18		Follow Channel 5 miles to Cedar Key Municipal Dock

When I originally planned this trip, we were going to go from Carrabelle to Suwannee River, and in fact that is what we did. We should have planned to go from Carrabelle to Cedar Key directly because that's where we ended up that night. The story is an interesting one. We arrived at the marina in Suwannee River at 5:00 p.m. The boat took 200 gallons, and since we only carry 240 gallons, we should have carried extra gas in Jerry cans to be safe. While we were gassing up, I mentioned to the man at the marina that the channel in the Suwannee River was very shallow at low tide since our depth meter showed we were in 4 feet of water and our boat draws 37 inches. The man said that this was high tide and the channel was only 1 foot deep at low tide. We checked the tide chart and found that we would be stranded there until the following afternoon. We decided to leave immediately and try to get to Cedar Key before dark, which was 16 miles south.

By the time we left, it was 6:00 p.m. and the channel was even shallower. I had to plane to raise the boat in the water. It is scary to plane at 18 miles per hour with 6 inches of water under the boat. We made it out of the Suwannee River into the Gulf without running aground but it was starting to get dark since it was January 27th. We ran the 11 miles to the Cedar Key Channel in the dark using GPS and following flashing buoys. From this point, we had to negotiate 5 miles of narrow channel to the Cedar Key Municipal dock. We had four people on board and everyone had a job. George Roth was at the helm; Helen Roth held a flashlight on the depth meter, which was the only gauge whose light was burnt out. My wife, Jeri, used the hand-held halogen light to spot channel markers, and I read the chart with a flashlight to identify channel markers and determine course headings. After successfully negotiating 4 miles of channel, we ran aground.

It was 8:00 p.m. when we ran aground. We checked the tide chart that we got in Suwannee River and saw that low tide was at 10:00 p.m. and the next high tide was at 4:00 a.m. We turned the generator on and then the lights and air conditioning. We had a nice dinner with wine after which we went to bed around 10:00 p.m. We set the alarm for 2:00 a.m. because we thought we would be floating by then. I got a very accurate fix with the GPS so I would know which way to move the boat once we were floating. Jeri got everyone up at 2:00 a.m. because we were floating. We moved the boat about 50 feet into the center of the channel and dropped anchor. We were now in 10 feet of water and we went back to bed.

Cedar Key Municipal Dock Phone: (352) 543-5132

Approach Depth	12'	Diesel Fuel	no
Dockside Depth	10'	Mechanical Repairs	no
Accepts Transients	yes	Ships Store	no
Dockside Power	no	Showers	no
Dockside Water	no	Laundromat	no
Gasoline	no	Restaurant	nearby

Cedar Key to Tarpon Springs, Florida

We got up with the sunrise at 7:00 a.m., we had 8 feet of water under the boat and it was a beautiful blue-sky day. We left at 8:00 a.m. and followed a boat in the channel out to the Gulf. There wasn't much wind and the ride was very smooth. We ran down the coast to Tarpon Springs and arrived there at 12:00 noon. We saw a number of Dolphins on our way and it was very relaxing, which was quite a contrast to the previous day, which was exciting but certainly not relaxing.

Tarpon Springs, Florida

Tarpon Springs is the northern end of the Gulf Intracoastal on the West Coast of Florida. From Tarpon Springs to Marco Island you have the choice of going inside or outside. Tarpon Springs is also the sponge capital of the USA. The original sponge divers who settled here were Greek. The town has a Greek flavor and a number of Greek restaurants. We visited the Sponge Diving Museum, saw the sponge and shrimp fleets and had dinner at Poppas Greek Restaurant. We stayed at Port Tarpon Marina, which also had a nice restaurant where we had lunch.

Port Tarpon Marina Phone: (813) 937-2200

Approach Depth	9'	**Diesel Fuel**	yes
Dockside Depth	9'	**Mechanical Repairs**	yes
Accepts Transients	yes	**Ships Store**	yes
Dockside Power	30,50	**Showers**	yes
Dockside Water	yes	**Laundromat**	no
Gasoline	yes	**Restaurant**	yes

Tarpon Springs to Longboat Key, Florida

We originally planned to go on the inside to Longboat Key, however, due to the nice weather we changed our mind and ran on the outside. At Longboat Inlet, we went inside and promptly ran aground. The Gulf Intracoastal on the West Coast of Florida is quite shallow and you can run aground if you get slightly out of the channel. Having learned my lesson in Biloxi, this time I called SeaTow. They pulled us off and the bill was $480 since the charge is based on the size of your boat. We continued on the inside to our marina the Longboat Key Moorings. This is a four-star facility that had swimming, tennis, an 18-hole golf course and an excellent restaurant in the marina. Longboat Key is a barrier island beach resort off of Sarasota, Florida. This is a nice place to stay for a few days, since it offers the cultural activities of Sarasota.

Longboat Key Mooring Marina Phone: (941) 383-8383

Approach Depth	7'	**Diesel Fuel**	yes
Dockside Depth	20'	**Mechanical Repairs**	no
Accepts Transients	yes	**Ships Store**	yes
Dockside Power	30,50,100	**Showers**	yes
Dockside Water	yes	**Laundromat**	yes
Gasoline	yes	**Restaurant**	yes

Longboat Key to Boca Grande, Florida

Our plan was to go inside to Venice Inlet and then go outside to Boca Grande. When we got to Venice Inlet we went outside, but it was very rough so we turned around and came back inside. We turned South on the Intracoastal, and within an hour, we ran aground again. We called SeaTow and this time it cost $430. The reason the charge was less than the previous day is that we had a different SeaTow franchise and apparently they each figure up the bill a little differently. I learned my lesson and the next day I called Boat/U.S., and for $88 per year, I bought unlimited towing insurance for a whole year. As a result of having towing insurance, we would run aground only one more time on the entire trip. We arrived at Millers Marina on Boca Grande at 5:00 p.m.

Millers Marina Phone: (941) 964-2283

Approach Depth	8'	**Diesel Fuel**	yes
Dockside Depth	8'	**Mechanical Repairs**	yes
Accepts Transients	yes	**Ships Store**	yes
Dockside Power	30,50	**Showers**	yes
Dockside Water	yes	**Laundromat**	yes
Gasoline	yes	**Restaurant**	yes

Boca Grande, Florida

Boca Grande is the only town on Gasparilla Island, which is an island north of Captiva on Florida's West Coast. This is a delightful island about 7 miles long and very uncrowded with a maximum population of 3,500 in high season (February through April). At the southern end of the island is Boca Grande Pass, which is world famous for Tarpon fishing in May and June. Fishermen come from all over the world to catch the hard fighting Tarpon, which can weigh several hundred pounds.   The island has a very relaxed atmosphere, uncrowded beaches, great fishing and a number of nice restaurants.   The island is also noted for its bridge toll, which is $3.25 to get onto the island, and it is free to get off.

We stayed on Boca Grande for five days since our friends George and Ann Lyons own a condo there. We rented a 19-ft. outboard one day and cruised around the many small islands around Boca Grande.   We saw many Dolphins plus white Pelican Island, which is a sandbar with several hundred all white Pelicans.   We went to Pine Island and had lunch at Bootleggers. Another day we rented a golf cart that holds four people and toured the island.

Boca Grande to Marco Island

We switched crews again at Boca Grande with our friends George and Helen Roth leaving and our oldest son, Bick, and our daughter-in-law, Kathy, joining us.   We had originally planned to go to Captiva for one night and then onto Marco Island from where we would make our 98-mile crossing to Key West.   The weather forecast called for a front to come through with some storm activity the following night.   We decided to skip Captiva and go right to Marco Island and make the crossing to Key West the next day ahead of the storm. We ran from Boca Grande to Marco Island in the Gulf, the water was flat, the sun was shining, and we had a beautiful ride. We stayed at the Marco River Marina, which was walking distance to a number of restaurants.

Marco River Marina Phone: (941) 472-5111

Approach Depth	6'	Diesel Fuel	yes
Dockside Depth	6'	Mechanical Repairs	yes
Accepts Transients	yes	Ships Store	yes
Dockside Power	30,50	Showers	yes
Dockside Water	yes	Laundromat	no
Gasoline	yes	Restaurant	nearby

Marco Island to Key West

We left Marco Island at 8:30 a.m. and arrived in Key West at 2:15 p.m. We had flat seas, but ran through two rain squalls each lasting about 30 minutes and we heard some thunder but didn't see any lightning. The route from Marco Island to Key West is as follows.

Points from Marco Island to Key West

Chart Book

Page 10A   Leaving Marco Island go to FL R "2" (25° 58.6'/81° 46.5')

C187   80.1 nm to G "1" (24° 38.8'/81° 54.0')

Page 14A   Follow channel from G "1" to G "5" which is the beginning of the Northwest channel. The Northwest Channel runs about 7 miles to G "15" at Key West Harbor.

Page 12A   At G "15" turn into Key West Harbor range C026 for about 1 mile to R "24". Take Key West right channel to Galleon Marina.

Key West

We really enjoyed Key West and we ended up staying there seven days. The Galleon Marina is the best place to stay because it is in the old town and is walking distance to everything. This was the most expensive marina that we stayed at on the entire trip ($2.25 per foot per day) however, it has all the amenities; swimming pool, sandy beach, etc. There are numerous shops, restaurants, and a lot of entertainment available in Key West. We took the bus tour of the island, had lunch at a sidewalk café called Mango's, and visited Hemingway's house. Another day, my son, Bick, and I rented scooters and toured the entire island. There are a number of museums in Key West, and one of the more interesting ones was Mel Fisher's Shipwreck Museum. One night we took a sunset cruise on a large sailboat. We had a number of good meals however, the best was at "Louie's Back Yard", which is open air on the Gulf.

It is interesting to note that Key West was the southern most point on our trip, whereas Mackinac Island was the northern most point. These two islands are both very interesting places to visit; however, they couldn't be more different.

Galleon Marina Phone: (305) 292-1292

Approach Depth	25'	**Diesel Fuel**	no
Dockside Depth	10'	**Mechanical Repairs**	yes
Accepts Transients	yes	**Ships Store**	yes
Dockside Power	30,50	**Showers**	yes
Dockside Water	yes	**Laundromat**	yes
Gasoline	no	**Restaurant**	yes

Nittany Navy in Gulf Intracoastal Waterway

Captain Bick Remmey navigating

Tarpin Springs, Florida — The Sponge Capital

The beach at Boca Grande, Florida

Our Marina at Key West

Crew No. 10 having dinner in Key West; Bick III, Jeri, Captain Bick and Kathy Remmey

Key West to West Palm Beach Intracoastal Waterway

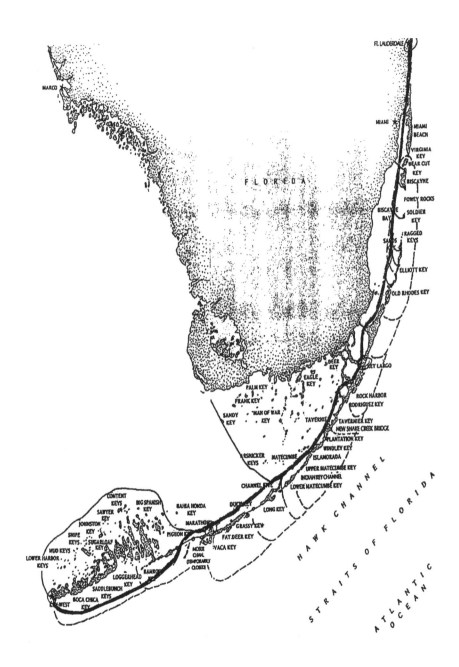

Distance (Statute Miles)

Destination	Between Points	Cumulative
Key West, FL	0	0
Marathon, FL	50	50
Key Largo, FL	59	109
Fort Lauderdale, FL	50	159
Delray Beach, FL	25	184
West Palm Beach, FL	20	204

Charts Required:
BBA Chart Kit – Florida's West Coast and The Keys
Chart #14F -- Pennekamp Park -Islamorada
BBA Chart Kit -- Jacksonville to Miami

Waterway Guide: *Waterway Guide - Southern*

Key West to Marathon

Our friends Jim and Betty Ann McArdle joined us in Key West
for the cruise through the Keys.

Key West to Marathon is approximately 50 statute miles with
the most direct route being the Hawk Channel. The Hawk
Channel runs along the Gulf side of the Keys between the
islands and outer reefs which make the channel smoother
than the Gulf itself but not as smooth as taking the inside
route. The inside route to Marathon has shallow water and
is longer. We had planned to leave Key West for Marathon via
the Hawk Channel on Tuesday, February 11, 1997; however,
it was windy and the Coast Guard had posted small craft
warnings. We decided to stay another day in Key West, which
was a good decision since the next day the winds had died
down and the weather was beautiful.

Our route to Marathon would follow the Hawk Channel for about 40 miles where we would go inside 10 miles south of Marathon so the last 10 miles would be on the ICW, after which, we would stay on the ICW all the way to New Jersey. Our route was as follows:

Reference BBA Chart Kit - Florida's West Coast and The Keys

Chart 12A	Follow Key West Harbor Channel South to Hawk Channel just before R "12" (SM1242) change course to 092
Chart 14A	Follow magenta course line to SM 1235
Chart 15A	Follow magenta course line to SM 1225
Chart 17A	Follow magenta course line (C082) to SM 1215
Chart 18A	Follow magenta course line to SM 1207.5 Waypoint 24° 37' 81° 17.5' Change course to 010 go under Bridge between Bahia Honda Key and Spanish Harbor Key to ICW at (SM 1205)
Chart 19A	Follow ICW to SM 1195 then to R "16" C 132 to Faro Blanco Marina (Lighthouse next to dock)

Marathon

Marathon is actually the city located on the island of Vaca Key, however, it is common for people to refer to the island as

Marathon. The island has a population of around 8,000 and has a hospital and an airport. Marathon also has many good restaurants plus quite a few motels and hotels. We stayed at the Faro Blanco Bayside Marina, which is known for its landmark lighthouse located next to the docks. This marina has a very nice swimming pool facility and an excellent restaurant.

Faro Blanco Bayside Marina Phone: (305) 743-9018

Approach Depth	7'	**Diesel Fuel**	yes
Dockside Depth	7'	**Mechanical Repairs**	no
Accepts Transients	yes	**Ships Store**	yes
Dockside Power	30,50	**Showers**	yes
Dockside Water	yes	**Laundromat**	yes
Gasoline	yes	**Restaurant**	yes

Marathon to Key Largo

The trip from Marathon to Key Largo is 59 miles following the ICW in Florida Bay. When leaving the marina, follow a course of C 005 to G "15A" [SM 1192] which is on the magenta course line on chart 20 A in the BBA Chart Kit. Continue to follow the magenta course line on charts 21 A, 22 A, 23 A to SM 1140. At this point you must switch to individual chart #14F. starting at SM 1140. Continue to follow the magenta course line to SM 1134, which is the marina. We left Marathon at 8:30 a.m. and arrived at our marina in Key Largo at 2:00 p.m.

Key Largo

Key Largo is 30 miles long and is home to the famous Ocean Reef Club. We stayed at Gilbert's Holiday Island at Key Largo

Marina, which is located on the ICW at the U.S. Route 1 Bridge where U.S. 1 crosses over from mainland Florida to the Keys. This marina is small but is very convenient to both the ICW and U.S. 1. The marina has a small swimming pool and a tiki bar. We took a cab to the Sundowners Restaurant in Key Largo and had a good meal.

Gilbert's Holiday Island at Key Largo Marina
Phone: (305) 451-1133

Approach Depth	10'	**Diesel Fuel**	yes
Dockside Depth	8'	**Mechanical Repairs**	no
Accepts Transients	yes	**Ships Store**	no
Dockside Power	30,50	**Showers**	yes
Dockside Water	yes	**Laundromat**	yes
Gasoline	yes	**Restaurant**	yes

Key Largo to Ft. Lauderdale

Our original plan was to go from Key Largo to Miami, however, the week that we were there was the week of the Miami boat show and there were no slips available in Miami. We were able to get a slip in Ft. Lauderdale so as a result we never got to stay in Miami on our boat, however, I have included a paragraph on Miami in this chapter.

You will recall that just before we arrived at Key Largo we had to switch to individual Chart #14 F instead of simply switching to the next BBA Chart Kit. The reason for this is that there are 30 miles missing between the two chart kits. Individual Chart #14 F includes this missing section which is between SM 1140 and SM 1110 on the ICW. Therefore, when you leave Key Largo, you are using individual Chart #14 F up to SM 1110. At this point, you switch to BBA Chart Kit --

Jacksonville to Miami Chart #27. SM 1110 is not shown but is at the bottom of the chart. Follow the magenta line on Charts 27 and 28 through Biscayne Bay to Miami. Chart 30 is where the marinas are for Miami and Miami Beach. Going north on the ICW Chart 29 comes after Chart 30 and the next chart after that is Chart 33. Our marina in Ft. Lauderdale was at SM 1064.5. The trip from Miami to Ft. Lauderdale is very slow, much of which is no wake zone. There are also many bridges including 4 or 5 that we couldn't get under and had to wait for the bridge opening. The good news is that although the trip is very slow here, the houses on either side of the waterway are so spectacular you want to slow down just to enjoy them.

Miami

Had we been able to stay in Miami, we planned to stay at the Miami Beach Marina, which is a very large, 400 slip capacity marina with every amenity nearby. Miami Beach is, of course, a large resort offering every type of entertainment, the best shopping, excellent restaurants, etc. The Miami Beach Marina is located on the main channel on the southern tip of the Miami Beach Island very close to the Ocean [Chart 30].

Ft. Lauderdale

Ft. Lauderdale is a virtual city of canals. You can go to stores and restaurants by boat. We stayed at the Bahia Mar Marina, which is beautifully located on the ICW and right next to the Beach. The marina is quite large and located next to the Raddison Hotel. There are several good restaurants in the hotel and several others within walking distance. This is a great place to stay if you would like to spend several days on the beach.

Bahia Mar Marina   Phone: (954) 764-2233

Approach Depth	12'	Diesel Fuel	yes
Dockside Depth	10'	Mechanical Repairs	no
Accepts Transients	yes	Ships Store	yes
Dockside Power	30,50,100	Showers	yes
Dockside Water	yes	Laundromat	yes
Gasoline	yes	Restaurant	yes

Ft. Lauderdale to Delray Beach

The trip from Ft. Lauderdale to Delray Beach is only 25 miles; however, it took us 3 hours because much of the way is "no wake" or "minimum wake" plus the many bridge openings. We were lucky, with our boat requiring 15 ft. 9 inch clearance, we were able to sneak under three 15 ft. bridges due to low tide. The bridge gauges were reading 16 ft. 5 inches at that time. The route from Ft. Lauderdale to Delray Beach is on Charts 33, 35 and 36. As with the trip from Miami to Ft. Lauderdale, this trip is also full of beautiful homes and beautiful boats on the waterway. It makes you wonder how so many people have that much money. We stayed at the Delray Beach Yacht Club [SM 1039] because it was close to Boca Raton where my mother spends the winters. Our friends Jim and Betty Ann McArdle flew home and we stayed with my mother for a week. If we were not visiting my mother, we would have skipped Delray Beach and gone directly from Ft. Lauderdale to West Palm Beach.

Delray Beach Yacht Club Phone: (407) 272-2700

Approach Depth	8'	Diesel Fuel	no
Dockside Depth	6'	Mechanical Repairs	no
Accepts Transients	yes	Ships Store	no
Dockside Power	30,50	Showers	yes

Dockside Water	yes	**Laundromat**	yes
Gasoline	no	**Restaurant**	no

Delray Beach to West Palm Beach

The distance from Delray Beach to West Palm Beach is only 20 miles [Charts 36 and 37]. The reason most people would go to Palm Beach is that it is a nice resort and is a good place to visit. We went there because it has a large airport (West Palm Beach Airport) and a number of boat yards where we could leave our boat for four months. Therefore, West Palm Beach was a convenient place for us to end the third leg of our trip and fly home. We left our boat at the Rybovich-Spencer Boatyard [SM 1019] and flew home on February 20, 1997.

Rybovich-Spencer Marina   Phone: (407) 844-1800

Approach Depth	9'	**Diesel Fuel**	yes
Dockside Depth	8'	**Mechanical Repairs**	yes
Accepts Transients	yes	**Ships Store**	yes
Dockside Power	30,50,100	**Showers**	yes
Dockside Water	yes	**Laundromat**	no
Gasoline	yes	**Restaurant**	no

Approaching Miami from Biscayne Bay

The ICW in Fort Lauderdale, Florida

West Palm Beach to Savannah Intracoastal Waterway

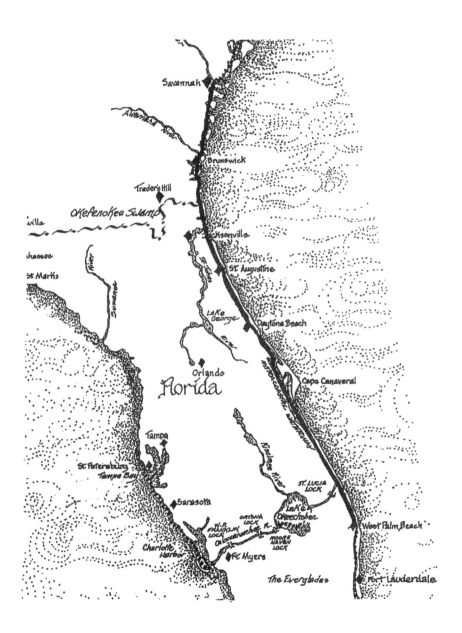

Distance (Statute Miles)

Destination	Between Points	Cumulative
West Palm Beach, FL	0	0
Vero Beach, FL	68	68
Titusville, FL	74	142
Daytona Beach, FL	47	189
St. Augustine, FL	53	242
Jacksonville Beach, FL	30	272
Jekyll Island, GA	64	336
Catherines Sound Area, GA	70	406
Savannah, GA	32	438

Charts Required:

BBA Chart Kit – Jacksonville to Miami

BBA Chart Kit - Norfolk to Jacksonville via ICW

Waterway Guide:

Waterway Guide - Southern

Waterway Guide - Mid-Atlantic

NOTE: The destinations where the author stayed are shown in bold type and are described in the following chapter. The other destinations are listed as intermediate ports if a shorter cruising day is desired. Check the waterway guide for information on intermediate ports.

West Palm Beach to Vero Beach

The 58-mile trip from Palm Beach to Vero Beach on the ICW is on Charts 37, 38, 39 and 41 in the BBA Chart Kit -- Jacksonville to Miami.

We flew from Philadelphia to West Palm Beach on May 13, 1997, to begin the fourth and final leg of the *Great Circle Cruise.* Our plan was to go to Vero Beach the next day and pick up Gene and Mildred Winne who would go with us to St. Augustine. We went to Vero Beach on the 14th, and on the 15th, we headed north with the Winnes onboard. At approximately 11:00 a.m., our port engine suddenly lost rpm and shut down. The nearest marina was three miles back, so we turned around and went there on one engine. A mechanic checked our engine and told us that it had blown a rod through the bottom of the block, split the oil pan, and dumped the oil into the bilge, after which the engine froze. We had traveled 4,000 miles without any engine problems, however, this made up for it since the engine was totaled. The engine was a 454 cubic inch, 350 Hp, V8 inboard with 1,150 hours on it. We made arrangements with the Complete Yacht Services Marina, in Vero Beach, to get a new engine and flew home.

On June 19th , Jeri and I flew back to West Palm Beach, rented a car, and drove back to Vero Beach to resume the boat trip. The people who had planned to go with us on this portion of the trip could not make it on the revised schedule, so Jeri and I would take the boat ourselves from Vero Beach to Baltimore. Our son, Chris, and his wife, Claudine, would join us there for the completion of our trip back to Avalon, New Jersey.

Complete Yacht Services Phone: (561) 231-2111

Approach Depth	6'	**Diesel Fuel**	yes
Dockside Depth	6'	**Mechanical Repairs**	yes
Accepts Transients	yes	**Ships Store**	yes
Dockside Power	30,50	**Showers**	yes

Dockside Water	yes	**Laundromat**	yes
Gasoline	yes	**Restaurant**	no

Vero Beach to Titusville

On June 21, 1997, we resumed our trip with one new engine and one old engine. We did the 74 miles from Vero Beach to Titusville in 5 hours. We had to hold the engine rpm down to 3,000 because we were breaking in the new engine. Since we normally cruise between 3,300 and 3,500 it took us a little longer than normal to make our destination. Using the BBA Chart Kit "Norfolk to Jacksonville via ICW", follow Charts 42, 43, 47 and 48 to Titusville. The Titusville Municipal Marina is at SM 878 just north of the Titusville swing bridge. NOTE: The Titusville Swing Bridge (vertical clearance 9 ft.) closes Monday through Friday 6:15 to 7:15 a.m. and 3 to 4:30 p.m.

Titusville

Titusville is the closest town to the Kennedy Space Center. If you have not visited the Kennedy Space Center, it is well worth your while to spend a day there. You can make arrangements at the marina to get transportation to the Space Center. Once there, a bus system transports you around from the visitor center complex to the space shuttle launch site, the Manned Space Exhibit and the Space Station Exhibit. Everything there is very well done. However, the Manned Space Exhibit, which features the Apollo Moon Program, is worth the trip all by itself. After visiting the Space Center, a great place to have dinner in Titusville is the Dixie Crossroads Restaurant, which features rock shrimp. This type of shrimp comes in a very hard shell, which requires a machine to split. This restaurant has invented that machine, and when you order, you get several dozen shrimp with their shells split open and swimming in butter.

Titusville Municipal Marina Phone: (407) 269-7258

Approach Depth	8'	Diesel Fuel	yes
Dockside Depth	8'	Mechanical Repairs	no
Accepts Transients	yes	Ships Store	yes
Dockside Power	30,50	Showers	yes
Dockside Water	yes	Laundromat	yes
Gasoline	yes	Restaurant	yes

Titusville to St. Augustine

The trip from Titusville to St. Augustine is 100 miles on the ICW starting at SM 878 at the Titusville Marina and ending at SM 778 at the St. Augustine Municipal Marina. You follow charts 48, 49, 51 (Daytona Beach), 52 and 53 to St. Augustine. Most of the ICW goes through wetlands between the mainland and barrier islands. This section is typical of this beautiful terrain, with many types of water birds such as Egrets, Herons, Pelicans, wild ducks, Sea Gulls, etc. The trip took 7 hours partially because of a number of no wake areas, however, the scenery was so beautiful that the seven hours went quickly.

St. Augustine

St. Augustine was founded in 1565 and is the oldest permanent European settlement in the United States. The St. Augustine Municipal Marina is located in the heart of the old city -- walking distance to almost everything. The fort, which has a moat, is only a 5 minutes walk from the Marina. Construction on the fort started in 1672. Across the street from the Marina is the A1A Brewery, which is a microbrewery and restaurant. The food here is quite good and very unusual since they serve no red meat. If you go there, try the cheese ale soup; it is excellent. We stayed in St. Augustine for three days and had a wonderful time. I would recommend the trolley tour, the movie at the Tourist Center, and the Lightner Museum along with the Fort and just walking around the old town.

St. Augustine Municipal Marina Phone: (904) 825-1026

Approach Depth	16'	**Diesel Fuel**	yes
Dockside Depth	16'	**Mechanical Repairs**	no
Accepts Transients	yes	**Ships Store**	yes
Dockside Power	30,50	**Showers**	yes
Dockside Water	yes	**Laundromat**	yes
Gasoline	yes	**Restaurant**	yes

St. Augustine to Jekyll Island

St. Augustine to Jekyll Island is 94 miles on the ICW and we made the trip in 6 hours and 45 minutes. Using the BBA Chart Kit - Jacksonville to Miami, the trip begins on Chart 53 at SM 778 and continues on Charts 54, 56, 57 and 58. On Chart 58 at SM 710, switch to BBA Chart Kit - Norfolk to Jacksonville Chart 38 at SM 710. The trip continues on Chart 37 and 36, which is Jekyll Island. The Jekyll Harbor Marina is at SM 684.

Jekyll Island

Jekyll Island was purchased in 1886 by a group of America's richest families as a private resort. The Rockefellers, Morgans and Vanderbilts all vacationed here. The state of Georgia purchased the island from the exclusive Jekyll Island Club in 1947. The island today is an elegant resort with a number of hotels and 63 holes of golf. One of the island attractions is a tour of the mansion-size "cottages" from the Jekyll Island Club era.

Jekyll Harbor Marina Phone: (912) 635-3137

Approach Depth	12'	**Diesel Fuel**	yes
Dockside Depth	10'	**Mechanical Repairs**	no
Accepts Transients	yes	**Ships Store**	yes
Dockside Power	30,50	**Showers**	yes
Dockside Water	yes	**Laundromat**	yes
Gasoline	yes	**Restaurant**	yes

Jekyll Island to Savannah

Jekyll Island to Savannah is 102 miles and we made the trip in 5.5 hours. Using the BBA Chart Kit - Norfolk to Jacksonville. Jekyll Island is on Chart 36 and the marina is at SM 684. Follow Charts 35, 34, 33, 32 and 32 to the Savannah Bend Marina at SM 582. The ICW only comes within 6 or 7 miles of downtown Savannah so that this marina is as convenient as any. At the time we were there, there were no marinas in downtown Savannah. We spent two days there and we took a cab into the city each day.

Savannah, Georgia

Neither Jeri nor I had ever been to Savannah before, so we were surprised by how much this city retains its original character. Savannah is a small city by today's standards, however, it is built around 21 squares which look like they haven't changed since before the civil war. The squares are basically small city parks with gardens surrounded by old elegant homes. The best way to see the squares is to take a trolley tour. Savannah also has a number of good restaurants. One in particular that we can recommend is the "Pink House". Savannah is also noted for its waterfront area located on the Savannah River. This area has been restored with interesting shops, restaurants, and Irish Pubs. There are a number of Irish Pubs which also have authentic Irish music. We were told that thousands of people come to Savannah every year for Saint Patrick's Day.

St. Augustine Municipal Marina Phone: (904) 825-1026

Approach Depth	13'	**Diesel Fuel**	yes
Dockside Depth	16'	**Mechanical Repairs**	no
Accepts Transients	yes	**Ships Store**	yes
Dockside Power	30,50	**Showers**	yes
Dockside Water	yes	**Laundromat**	yes
Gasoline	yes	**Restaurant**	yes

The Fort at St. Augustine, Florida

A house on one of the beautiful squares in Savannah, Georgia

Savannah to Norfolk
Intracoastal Waterway

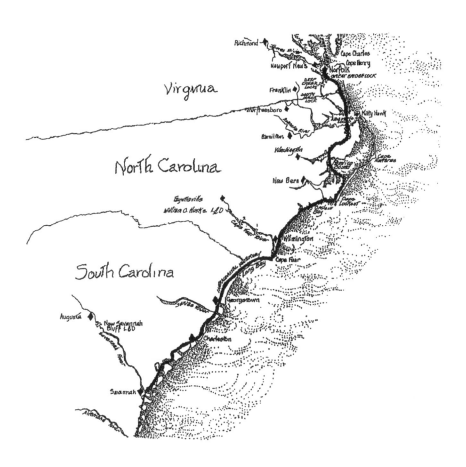

Distance (Statute Miles)

Destination	Between Points	Cumulative
Savannah, GA	0	0
Beaufort, SC	46	46
Charleston, SC	67	113
Georgetown, SC	74	187
Southport, NC	75	262
Wrightsville, Beach, NC	37	299
Morehead, City Basin, NC	79	378
Belhaven, NC	68	446
Coinjock, NC	87	533
Norfolk, VA	49	582

Charts Required:
BBA Chart Kit – Norfolk, VA to Jacksonville, FL

Waterway Guide: *Waterway Guide - Mid-Atlantic*

NOTE: The destinations where the author stayed are shown in bold type and are described in the following chapter. The other destinations are listed as intermediate ports if a shorter cruising day is desired. Check the waterway guide for information on intermediate ports.

Savannah to Charleston

We did the entire 113-mile trip from Savannah to Charleston in 6.5 hours. We did not stop in Beaufort; however, it looked like a nice town, and had we had more time, we would have stayed there. Using BBA Chart Kit -- Norfolk to Jacksonville, follow Chart 31 from Savannah to Chart 30, 29 (Beaufort), 28, 27 and 26 to Charleston. This entire trip is pretty much through wetlands and is quite beautiful. We stayed at the

Charleston City Marina, which is new and very nice. This marina has a great location since the tour buses stop there, the water tour boats dock there, and there are several restaurants including Pussers, which is very good.

Charleston

Charleston was founded in 1670 by the British. By the time that Washington was president, Charleston was the fourth largest city in the United States with only Philadelphia, New York and Boston being larger. During the pre-civil war days, the wealthy plantation owners would build houses in Charleston to escape the summer heat inland. The unique architecture of these Charleston homes was designed to catch the maximum amount of sea breeze by having a side porch that the wind could pass through instead of a front porch which would block the wind. These houses often had a fake front door since the real door was off of the side porch.

We would recommend a bus tour of the historic district including some of the elegant homes. The visitors' center has a movie of the history of Charleston, which is worthwhile. They have boat tours to Fort Sumter the shelling of which was the beginning of the civil war. Charleston is also known for its wonderful restaurants including the South Bend Brewery and Hymans Seafood. Hymans Seafood Restaurant is really outstanding and deserves the line of people on the sidewalk outside waiting to get in.

Charleston City Marina Phone: (803) 723-5098

Approach Depth	10'	Diesel Fuel	no
Dockside Depth	10'	Mechanical Repairs	no
Accepts Transients	yes	Ships Store	yes

Dockside Power	30,50	**Showers**	yes
Dockside Water	yes	**Laundromat**	yes
Gasoline	no	**Restaurant**	yes

Charleston to Georgetown

The trip from Charleston to Georgetown is 66 miles, however, we went another 8 miles to stay at the Heritage Plantation Marina because our friends Jim and Carol Davies lived near there. The Heritage Plantation also includes a beautiful 18-hole golf course, which is open to the public. This would be a good place to stay if you want to play golf, otherwise you might want to stay at a marina in Georgetown. Following the Norfolk to Jacksonville Chart Kit, Charleston is on Chart 26, after which you follow Charts 25, 24 and 23 to Georgetown and the Heritage Plantation Marina.

Heritage Plantation Marina Phone: (803) 237-3650

Approach Depth	30'	**Diesel Fuel**	no
Dockside Depth	30'	**Mechanical Repairs**	no
Accepts Transients	yes	**Ships Store**	no
Dockside Power	30,50	**Showers**	yes
Dockside Water	yes	**Laundromat**	yes
Gasoline	no	**Restaurant**	no

Georgetown to Southport

From Georgetown to Southport the ICW winds through the wetlands between barrier islands and the mainland. The trip is 75 miles and there are a number of slow areas and many bridges, which require opening. We left Georgetown at 8:15 a.m. and arrived at our marina near Southport at 2:15 p.m. Using the BBA Chart Kit -- Norfolk to Jacksonville, follow Charts 23, 22, 21 and 20 to the marina at SM 320. We stayed at the Blue Water Point Marina, which is next to the Beach. We had dinner at the Fish House Restaurant, which was in the marina.

Blue Water Point Marina Phone: (910) 278-1230

Approach Depth	5'	Diesel Fuel	yes
Dockside Depth	5'	Mechanical Repairs	no
Accepts Transients	yes	Ships Store	yes
Dockside Power	30,50	Showers	yes
Dockside Water	yes	Laundromat	no
Gasoline	yes	Restaurant	yes

Southport to Morehead City

We did the 116-mile trip from Southport to Morehead City in 8 hours. We did not stay in Wrightsville Beach but chose to go all the way to Morehead City. We left at 7:10 a.m. and arrived at 3:15 p.m. We had to wait for three bridge openings and the worst was a pontoon bridge where we waited 40 minutes. Using the BBA Chart Kit, follow Charts 20, 19, 18 (Wrightsville Beach), 17, 16 and 15 to Morehead City. We stayed at the Morehead City Yacht Basin Marina (SM 204).

Morehead City

We stayed in Morehead City because we have several friends who own condos in Atlantic Beach, which is across the bridge from Morehead City. We stayed with one of them while we were there. You can choose to stay in Morehead City or Beaufort, which is right next to Morehead City and both towns are on the ICW. If you choose Beaufort, the marinas are in the waterfront area, which has many nice shops and restaurants within walking distance. If you stay in Morehead

City, you might want to rent a car to visit Fort Macon, which is on the north end of Bogue Bank Island and was used in the civil war. Also, if you had a car, you could go to the beach at Atlantic Beach and visit Beaufort.

Morehead City Yacht Basin Marina Phone: (919) 726-6862

Approach Depth	12'	**Diesel Fuel**	yes
Dockside Depth	8'	**Mechanical Repairs**	yes
Accepts Transients	yes	**Ships Store**	yes
Dockside Power	30,50	**Showers**	yes
Dockside Water	yes	**Laundromat**	yes
Gasoline	yes	**Restaurant**	yes

Morehead City to Belhaven

All the way from Miami, the ICW runs very close to the Atlantic Ocean. However, at Morehead City, the ICW goes inland via canal to the Neuse River. The ICW then follows the Western Shore of Pamlico Sound to the Pungo River to Belhaven. Whereas Morehead City was a few miles from the Beach, Belhaven is about 60 miles east of the Beach, which is now on Hatteras Island on the southern end of the Outer Banks. Follow the BBA Chart Kit on Chart 15 into the canal, and then on Chart 14, follow the canal to the Neuse River. Once in the Neuse River, follow the ICW magenta course line on Charts 14, 13 and 12. Follow the canal on Chart 11, then cross the Pamlico River to Chart 10. On Chart 10, cruise up the Pungo River to Belhaven.

We stayed at the River Forest Marina in Belhaven, which is a B & B in an old southern mansion with pillars. They have a restaurant there which features a buffet. They also have a nice bar and a swimming pool. The day we stayed there was

July 4, 1997, and we watched the fireworks from our boat. This was the second 4th of July that we spent on our boat trip. July 4, 1996, we were on Mackinac Island, MI.

River Forest Marina Phone: (919) 943-2151

Approach Depth	10'	**Diesel Fuel**	yes
Dockside Depth	10'	**Mechanical Repairs**	yes
Accepts Transients	yes	**Ships Store**	yes
Dockside Power	30,50	**Showers**	yes
Dockside Water	yes	**Laundromat**	yes
Gasoline	yes	**Restaurant**	yes

Belhaven to Coinjock

The trip from Belhaven to Coinjock is 87 miles long. Using the BBA Chart Kit, follow Charts 10 and 9 (Alligator River Canal) to Chart 8 (Alligator River) to Chart 7 (Albemarle Sound). On Chart 7 you will see that there are two routes across the Sound. One course takes you to the Dismal Swamp Canal and the other course goes to the Virginia Cut Canal. The Virginia Cut Canal is the primary ICW route. The Dismal Swamp Canal is shorter in miles but is known for floating debris. Both canal routes come together south of Norfolk. We chose the Virginia Cut route, which goes to Coinjock.

The Albemarle Sound has a reputation for being the roughest piece of water on the ICW. The reason for this is that it is shallow and is protected from the Atlantic Ocean only by the Outer Banks, which are only sandbars. Winds coming from the Ocean can whip up 6-ft. waves on the Sound, and due to the shallow water the waves are very close together. This condition can pound a boat severely. My recommendation when crossing the Albemarle Sound is to wait for a good weather forecast. When we crossed the Sound we had only 3-ft. waves, however, it was pretty rough. On Chart 7, follow the ICW magenta line across the Sound. The next chart is Chart 3, which takes you into a canal and onto Coinjock, which is on the canal. We stayed at the Midway Marina, which does not have a restaurant, however, they lent us a car so we could drive to one.

About 30 minutes out of Belhaven, I learned a lesson. Since the ICW has very calm water almost all the way, I left the TV and all the lamps up while we traveled. When cruising in the Ocean, Gulf, Great Lakes, etc. where we can have rough water, I put the TV and lamps on the floor so they can't fall off. What happened 30 minutes out of Belhaven was that we ran aground going full speed at 18 knots in the Alligator canal. The TV and the lamps flew through the air, and somehow, none of them were broken. The refrigerator door flew open and all the contents flew out. Magazines and any items on a counter surface also became airborne. We were very lucky to have so little damage. We had towing insurance with Boat U.S. and they pulled us off within 30 minutes. However, the lesson I learned is when cruising, prepare the boat for rough water even if your course should be very smooth.

Midway Marina Phone: (919) 453-3625

Approach Depth	12'	**Diesel Fuel**	yes
Dockside Depth	10'	**Mechanical Repairs**	yes
Accepts Transients	yes	**Ships Store**	yes
Dockside Power	30,50	**Showers**	yes
Dockside Water	yes	**Laundromat**	yes
Gasoline	yes	**Restaurant**	no

Coinjock to Norfolk

The trip from Coinjock to Norfolk is 49 miles. Using the BBA Chart Kit-Chart No. 3, follow the canal to the Currituck Sound and then to Chart 2 and the North Landing River to the Albemarle and Chesapeake Canal, which has one lock. The canal continues on Chart 1 where it connects with the South Elizabeth River. Follow the South Elizabeth River into Norfolk Harbor. The Waterside Marina is at Town Point (Chart 1, Insert A) at ICW SM 000. The last few miles of the South Elizabeth River and Norfolk Harbor has the largest concentration of naval ships that I have ever seen. There were submarines, cruisers, destroyers, two carriers and many other types of Navy ships. I would guess that there were between 50 and 100 Navy ships there.

Norfolk

The Norfolk Waterfront at Town Point has been rebuilt similar to Baltimore Inner Harbor. The Rouse Company, who rebuilt Baltimore Inner Harbor, also rebuilt the Norfolk Waterfront. The Waterfront Marina is part of the complex, which includes 100 shops and restaurants. Just like Baltimore Inner Harbor, they often have free outside entertainment.

Waterside Marina Phone: (757) 625-2000

Approach Depth	40'	**Diesel Fuel**	yes
Dockside Depth	20'	**Mechanical Repairs**	no
Accepts Transients	yes	**Ships Store**	yes
Dockside Power	30,50,100	**Showers**	yes
Dockside Water	yes	**Laundromat**	yes
Gasoline	no	**Restaurant**	yes

One of the many beautiful pre-Civil War homes in Charleston, South Carolina

A treasure hunting boat docked at the Heritage Plantation Marina, South Carolina

The B & B at the River Forest Marina in Belhaven, North Carolina

A carrier docked in Norfolk Harbor

Norfolk to the C & D Canal
The Chesapeake Bay

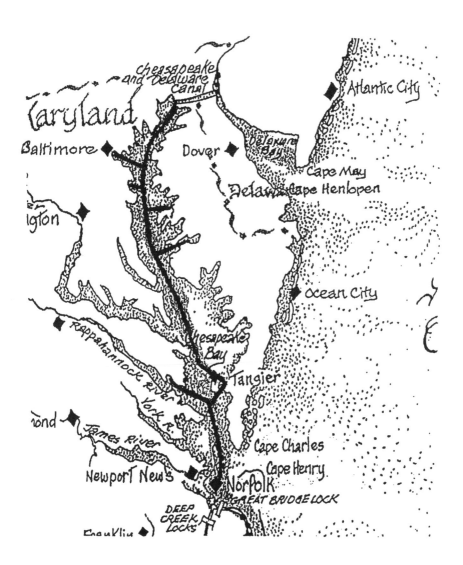

Destination	Distance (Statute Miles) Between Points	Cumulative
Norfolk, VA	0	0
Irvington, VA (Tides Inn)	60	60
Tangier Island & Crisfield, MD	51	111
Cambridge, MD	77	188
St. Michaels, MD	46	234
Annapolis, MD	29	263
Baltimore, MD	31	294
Chesapeake City, MD (C & D Canal)	54	348

Charts Required:
Chesapeake Bay Chart Book

Waterway Guide:
Waterway Guide - Southern

The Chesapeake Bay

The Chesapeake Bay is truly a cruising paradise with 4,000 miles of coastline and countless destinations. The Bay is 200 miles long and approximately 20 miles wide. The average depth is 20 feet and the water changes from salt water in the Southern Bay to brackish water in mid-Bay to fresh water in the Northern Bay. Destinations vary from large cities: Norfolk, Washington D.C., Baltimore and Annapolis to small towns such as St. Michaels, Cambridge, Rockhall to numerous gunkholes. The huge number of rivers and creeks that flow into the Chesapeake provide countless anchorages in quiet protected water. Since we keep our boat in Avalon, New Jersey, we can get to the Chesapeake in approximately

5 hours.   As a result of this, we have had 8 different
Chesapeake Cruises, all of which were different.

Norfolk to Irvington, VA (Tides Inn)

Since the Chesapeake has a lot of shallow areas, I normally
follow the blue course lines in the Chesapeake Chart Book as
long as they are going where I want to go. I also use the GPS
to guide me from waypoint to waypoint. The course from
Norfolk to Tides Inn is as follows:

Chart 15	Start G "3" (36° 58.4' -- 76° 19.7')	
	C063	2.8 nm to G "21"
	C021	5.5 nm to G "1BR" (37° 05.6' -- 76° 14.9')
Chart 14	C021	20 nm to Wolf Trap 52 ft. (37° 23.5' -- 76° 11.4')
Chart 13	C010	11 nm to RN "2R" (37° 34.2' -- 76° 11.6')
	C289	6.5 nm to G "7R"
Chart 27	Follow Rappahannoch River for approximately 9 miles to Tides Inn (Location 2 - E on Chart)	

Tides Inn

Tides Inn is a four star resort where you can stay on your
boat and enjoy all their facilities. The Tides Inn has two golf
courses, tennis courts, two restaurants, a sandy beach, and
a large swimming pool area. This is a great place to stay for
several days for a change of pace.

Tides Inn Marina Phone: (804) 438-5000

Approach Depth	6'	**Diesel Fuel**	no
Dockside Depth	6'	**Mechanical Repairs**	no
Accepts Transients	yes	**Ships Store**	yes
Dockside Power	30,50	**Showers**	yes
Dockside Water	yes	**Laundromat**	yes
Gasoline	no	**Restaurant**	no

Irvington, VA to Tangier Island

The trip from Tides Inn to Tangier Island is 40 statute miles and the route is as follows:

Chart 27	Follow Rappahannock River 9 miles to G "7R"
Chart 13	C109 6.5 nm to RN "2R" C039 5.8 nm to R "58" (37° 39.4' -- 76° 08')
Chart 11	C054 11 nm to Tangier Sound (45') C024 2.7 nm to GC "3" C326 .7 nm to Tangier Channel at G "1"

Tangier Island

Tangier Island is an island in the Chesapeake Bay that was first settled 300 years ago by the English. The 550 people who live there still have an old English accent. The Island has a small airport for private planes but is mainly connected to the mainland by ferry. The Island did not have electricity until after World War II. There is no local government, so order is maintained by family rule, town fathers, and the

Methodist Church. The Methodist Church is the only church on the Island. The Islanders make a living by crabbing and specialize in soft-shell crabs. They have a school on the Island, which is kindergarten through 12th grade. The year we were there, our guide told us that their school had graduated nine students that year and all nine were accepted into college. The Island has only one village, which looks like a New England fishing village. Next to the Methodist Church is a graveyard where the stone caskets are above ground because the water level is only 2 feet below the surface.

Eleven miles north of Tangier Island is Smith Island, which is very similar. The main difference between Smith Island and Tangier Island is that Smith Island is in Maryland and Tangier Island is in Virginia.

Tangier Island to Crisfield, VA

The trip from Tangier Island to Crisfield is only 11 statute miles. The route is as follows:

Chart 11   Follow Channel Back to G "1"
                        C146 .7 nm to GC "3"
                        C034 1.3 nm to G "5"
                        C017 2.9 nm to R "6"

Chart 10   C032 3.5 nm to GC "1"
                        Follow Channel into Crisfield

Crisfield, VA

Crisfield is known as the Crab Capital of the World. The town was originally settled by farmers in the 1600's, and in the 1800's it became the oyster fishing center. However, oystering has declined over the last 40 years and the Blue Crab has become more abundant and the major business of Crisfield. Next to the state Marina there are grandstands set up to watch the annual crab races. Crisfield is a nice place to visit on a boat because everything is in walking distance. There are a number of good restaurants there where you can have the best crab cakes in the world.

Somers Cove Marina Phone: (410) 968-0925

Approach Depth	10'	**Diesel Fuel**	yes
Dockside Depth	10'	**Mechanical Repairs**	no
Accepts Transients	yes	**Ships Store**	no
Dockside Power	30,50	**Showers**	yes
Dockside Water	yes	**Laundromat**	yes
Gasoline	yes	**Restaurant**	no

Crisfield, VA to Cambridge, MD

The trip from Crisfield to Cambridge is 77 statute miles long. Using the Chesapeake Bay Chart Book, the route is as follows:

Chart 10	Follow Channel out of Crisfield to GC "1"
	C300 .6 nm to R "8"
	C029 2.2 nm to G "9"
	C319 4.8 nm to G "5"
	C295 1.9 nm to R "4"
	C286 1.1 nm to R "2"
Chart 9	C307 8.4 nm to R "72"
Chart 7	C358 5.8 nm to RW "HS"
	C343 7.1 nm to RW "HI"

C353 9.9 nm to RW "CP"

Chart 6   C002 3.9 nm to R "2"
                        C015 3.0 nm to G "3"
                        C059 2.2 nm to R "6"
                        C051 3.0 nm to R "10"
                        C103 6.0 nm to R "14"
                        C133 1.0 nm to R "16"
                        C111 1.1 nm to R "18"
                        C164 1.4 nm to G "19"

Chart 3   Follow Choptank River Channel to
                        Cambridge

Cambridge, MD

Cambridge was founded in the 1600's and has been a seaport
ever since. The marinas are located near the Cambridge
Creek. We stayed at the Cambridge Yacht Club, which was a
very nice facility with a good restaurant. A few blocks from
the Yacht Club is Historic High Street, and the downtown
shops are a few blocks beyond that. Clayton's Restaurant is
a popular place to eat.

Cambridge Yacht Club Marina Phone: (410) 228-2141

Approach Depth	8'	**Diesel Fuel**	no
Dockside Depth	8'	**Mechanical Repairs**	no
Accepts Transients	yes	**Ships Store**	no
Dockside Power	30,50	**Showers**	yes
Dockside Water	yes	**Laundromat**	no
Gasoline	yes	**Restaurant**	yes

Cambridge to St. Michaels

The trip from Cambridge to St. Michaels is 46 statute miles. Using the Chesapeake Bay Chart Book, the route is as follows:

Chart 3	Follow Choptank River Channel to G "19"
Chart 6	C354 1.4 nm to R "18"
	C291 1.1 nm to R "16"
	C313 1.0 nm to R "14"
	C283 6.0 nm to R "10"
	C281 5.2 nm to RW "CR"
Chart 5	C359 6.3 nm to G "83"
	C052 5.3 nm to G "1"
	C075 3.3 nm to R "2A"
	C061 3.2 nm to R "4"
	C140 .4 nm to R "6"
	C168 1.9 nm to R "8"
	C163 2.1 nm to R "12"
	Follow Channel into St. Michaels

St. Michaels, MD

St. Michaels is probably the most popular destination on the Eastern Shore. It is a delightful town with many shops and restaurants as well as the Chesapeake Bay Maritime Museum. The museum is well worth a visit and includes a lighthouse, which was moved to the museum as one of the exhibits. There are two marinas: the St. Michaels Harbor Inn and the St. Michaels Town Dock Marina. Both marinas have swimming pools and restaurants, however, the Town Dock

Marina is a shorter walk to town. St. Michaels is a place where you can spend several days enjoying the Eastern Shore experience.

St. Michaels Town Dock Marina Phone: (800) 678-8980

Approach Depth	10'	**Diesel Fuel**	yes
Dockside Depth	9'	**Mechanical Repairs**	no
Accepts Transients	yes	**Ships Store**	yes
Dockside Power	30,50	**Showers**	yes
Dockside Water	yes	**Laundromat**	yes
Gasoline	yes	**Restaurant**	yes

St. Michaels to Annapolis

The cruise from St. Michaels to Annapolis is only 29 miles. The route is as follows:

Chart 5	Follow Channel to R "12"
	C343 2.1 nm to R "8"
	C348 1.9 nm to R "6"
	C335 .4 nm to R "4"
	C241 3.2 nm to R "2A"
	C255 3.3 nm to G "1"
	C310 1.4 nm to Bloody Point Bar Light
	C314 3.2 nm to G "1"
	C034 2.0 nm to GRC "SR"
Chart 4	C013 2.3 nm to G "1AH"
	C353 1.2 nm to R "4"
	C325 1.2 nm to R "8"
	Follow Channel to Annapolis Harbor

Annapolis, MD

Annapolis is my favorite boating destination. It has everything, great restaurants, entertainment, history, sightseeing, beautiful colonial buildings and everything is walking distance from the marina. There is a water taxi, which takes you anywhere for 1 dollar. Annapolis is the state capital of Maryland and the historic capital building is only a few blocks from the waterfront. Many of the streets around the capital are cobblestone and the buildings are original from colonial times. The Naval Academy is adjacent and is well worth a tour.

We always stay at the Annapolis Yacht Basin, which is next to the Annapolis Yacht Club and overlooks the Naval Academy. If you belong to a Yacht Club, the Annapolis Yacht Club will give you a guest pass so you can have dinner there. The Yacht Club dining room is on the top floor and overlooks the Annapolis Harbor, which is quite beautiful with many boats moored in the Harbor. On the other side of the marina is the Marriott Hotel, which has waterfront outdoor dining facing the famous "Ego Alley". Ego Alley is a narrow strip of water with shops and restaurants on either side where people bring their boats into a dead end and then turn around and go back out.

Annapolis Yacht Basin Marina Phone: (410) 263-3544

Approach Depth	15'	**Diesel Fuel**	yes
Dockside Depth	15'	**Mechanical Repairs**	no
Accepts Transients	yes	**Ships Store**	yes
Dockside Power	30,50,100	**Showers**	yes
Dockside Water	yes	**Laundromat**	yes
Gasoline	yes	**Restaurant**	no

Annapolis to Baltimore Inner Harbor

The distance from Annapolis to Baltimore Inner Harbor is 31 statute miles. Using the Chesapeake Bay Chart Book, the route is as follows:

Chart 4   Follow the Annapolis Channel to R "6"
                       C085 3.7 nm to R "92" (in front of
                            bridge)
                       C250 1.1 nm to R "94"
                       C015 1.5 nm to G "1C"
                       C353 1.7 nm to G "5"
                       C355 1.4 nm to G "9"
                       C011 2.7 nm to R "16"
                       C351 1.4 nm to R "20"

Chart 2   C343 2.7 nm to R "2B"
                       C300 3.5 nm to G "15"
                       Follow Baltimore Channel

Chart 34   Follow West Channel to Baltimore Inner
                       Harbor

Baltimore Inner Harbor

Baltimore Inner Harbor is my second favorite destination to Annapolis. You will want to stay in the Inner Harbor Marina of Baltimore, which is right in the Inner Harbor. The marina office and ships store is in the same building with the Rusty Scupper Restaurant. Since this destination is so popular, you will have to make reservations for the marina several weeks in advance. The Inner Harbor has many restaurants and hundreds of shops plus outside entertainment. The National Aquarium is a "must see". A boat ride to historic

Fells Point and Fort McHenry are also recommended. If you are a baseball fan, you are in walking distance to Camden Yards where the Baltimore Orioles play in what many say is the best baseball stadium in the country. Baltimore Inner Harbor also has an IMAX show and the frigate Constellation, which was launched in 1797, which you can visit.

Inner Harbor Marina of Baltimore   Phone: (410) 837-1834

Approach Depth	40'	**Diesel Fuel**	yes
Dockside Depth	25'	**Mechanical Repairs**	no
Accepts Transients	yes	**Ships Store**	yes
Dockside Power	30,50	**Showers**	yes
Dockside Water	yes	**Laundromat**	yes
Gasoline	yes	**Restaurant**	yes

Baltimore Inner Harbor to Chesapeake City (C & D Canal)

The trip from Baltimore Inner Harbor to Chesapeake City is 54 statute miles. Following the Chesapeake Chart Book, the route is as follows:

Chart 34	Follow Channel past Fort McHenry
Chart 2	Follow Channel to G "15"
	C120 3.5 nm to R "2B"
	C062 3.8 nm to G "1"
	C083 2.2 nm to R "4"
	C065 1.1 nm to R "6"
	C052 5.4 nm to R "40"
	C045 .4 nm to R "42"
	C058 2.7 nm to R "50"
	C068 2.4 nm to R "54

Chart 1   C073 1.4 nm to R "56"
                             C077 3.3 nm to G "IER" (Elk River)
                             C054 5.4 nm to R "12"
                             C059 3.2 nm to R "18"
                             Follow Channel into C & D Canal and
                             Chesapeake City

Chesapeake City (C & D Canal)

The C & D Canal originally opened in 1829 to link the Chesapeake Bay with the Delaware River. Chesapeake City was originally built to house the workers who built the Canal. During the civil war, Union forces were stationed here to make sure that the Confederate Army did not blow up the Canal. The Canal was rebuilt in the early 1900's to eliminate the locks and to permit large boats to pass through. Today, the 12-mile long Canal is 450 feet wide and 35 feet deep, which permits large ocean going ships to use the Canal. Free dockage is available at government wharf in Chesapeake City however, it is better to anchor out. The Bayard House Restaurant is the place to eat with a view of the Canal. On the opposite side of the Canal from Chesapeake City is Schaefer's Canal House, which has transients slips, fuel, and a large restaurant.

Schaefer's Canal House Marina Phone: (410) 885-2204

Approach Depth	36'	**Diesel Fuel**	yes
Dockside Depth	14'	**Mechanical Repairs**	no
Accepts Transients	yes	**Ships Store**	yes
Dockside Power	30,50	**Showers**	yes
Dockside Water	yes	**Laundromat**	no
Gasoline	yes	**Restaurant**	yes

A Chesapeake Bay lighthouse

Tides Inn on The Rappahannock River

Nittany Navy at Baltimore Inner Harbor

Crew No. 13 at Baltimore Inner Harbor; Jeri, Chris and Claudine Remmey

C & D Canal to New York City
Delaware Bay and the
New Jersey Shore

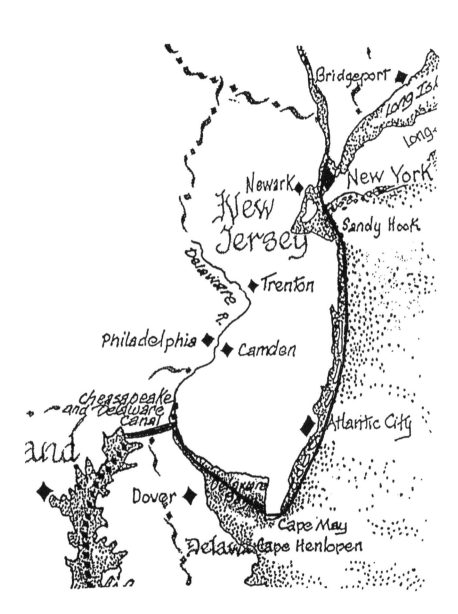

Destination	Distance (Statute Miles) Between Points	Cumulative
Chesapeake City, MD	0	0
Cape May, NJ	69	69
Atlantic City, NJ	41	110
Brielle, NJ	57	167
New York City	44	211

Charts Required:
NOAA Charts - 12311, 12304, 12316, 12324, 12327

Waterway Guide: *Waterway Guide - Northern*

The Chesapeake Bay to Cape May, New Jersey

The trip from Chesapeake City to Cape May, New Jersey is 69 statute miles. Follow the C & D Canal for 12 miles to the Delaware River. Using NOAA charts 12311 and 12304, follow the main ship channel, which is well marked. You will pass close by three lighthouses. The first lighthouse is the "Ship John Light" at (N 39° 18.3' -- W 75° 22.5'). The second lighthouse is the "Cross Ledge Light" at (N 39° 11' -- W 75° 16.1'), and the third lighthouse is the "Mia Maull Light" at (N 39° 7.5' -- W 75° 12.5'). At the Mia Maull Light you leave the main ship channel on a course of 142 deg. for 17 nautical miles to the entrance of the Cape May Canal (N 38° 58' -- W 74° 58'). Follow the Cape May Canal 3.2 miles to Cape May Harbor.   The Canyon Club Marina is on your left immediately after passing under the bridge.

Cape May, New Jersey

Cape May, New Jersey probably has the largest number of

Victorian houses in any one place. Many of the Victorian homes are B & B's offering bed and breakfast in a Victorian setting. Cape May is also known for its many good restaurants. Some of the best restaurants are the Washington Inn, Peaches Sunset, the Ebbett Room in the Virginia Hotel, and the Mad Batter. If you are staying in the Canyon Club Marina, take a taxi to the boardwalk area and take a leisurely walk up and down the many streets with nothing but Victorian gingerbread houses. Another popular way to see this unique town is by horse drawn carriage.

Canyon Club Marina Phone: (609) 884-0199

Approach Depth	6'	**Diesel Fuel**	yes
Dockside Depth	6'	**Mechanical Repairs**	yes
Accepts Transients	yes	**Ships Store**	yes
Dockside Power	30,50	**Showers**	yes
Dockside Water	yes	**Laundromat**	no
Gasoline	yes	**Restaurant**	no

Cape May to Atlantic City

The trip from Cape May to Atlantic City is 41 statute miles. The simplest way to make this trip is in the ocean running about 2 miles off of the beach. There is an Intracoastal Waterway in New Jersey, however it has some problems. The inland waterway is very shallow in the Wildwood area, and there are so many bridges in the Atlantic City area that have to open, it is usually much easier to go outside. Using NOAA chart 12316, cruise up the coast to the Atlantic City Inlet (N 39° 21.1' -- W 74° 23.7'). Enter the inlet and about 1.5 miles in you will see the Frank Farley State Marina on the left and a little further is the Harrah's Casino Marina. The Frank Farley State Marina is next to the Trump Castle Casino.

Therefore, the marina that you stay at depends on your Casino choice. We stayed at Harrah's.

Atlantic City

Atlantic City has had a rebirth with the coming of all the casinos. Compared to Las Vegas, there are not very many casinos in Atlantic City, only 14; however, they are very large. Even if you don't gamble, the casino marinas are a great place to stay because the marinas offer many restaurants and lots of entertainment at reasonable prices. The cheapest hotel room in Harrah's Casino Hotel is probably $200, however, the marina only charges $35 for a 40-ft. boat slip and you can order room service on your boat.

Harrah's Casino Marina   Phone: (609) 441-5315

Approach Depth	25'	**Diesel Fuel**	no
Dockside Depth	15'	**Mechanical Repairs**	no
Accepts Transients	yes	**Ships Store**	no
Dockside Power	30,50	**Showers**	yes
Dockside Water	yes	**Laundromat**	yes
Gasoline	no	**Restaurant**	yes

Atlantic City to Brielle, New Jersey

The trip from Atlantic City to Brielle, New Jersey, which is at the Manasquan Inlet is 57 statute miles running on the outside and about 70 miles on the inside. The inside route includes the Barnegat Bay and there are a lot of "no wake" areas. If the weather is nice, I recommend the outside route running several miles off of the beach. Using the NOAA charts 12316 and 12324 cruise up the coast to Manasquan Inlet. The Manasquan Inlet buoy is R "2M" at (N 40° 05.5' --

W 74° 00.8'). Go into the Manasquan Inlet and the marinas are about 1 mile in. We stayed at the Brielle Yacht Club, which has a nice facility. There are several restaurants right there.

Brielle Yacht Club Marina Phone: (908) 528-6250

Approach Depth	12'	**Diesel Fuel**	yes
Dockside Depth	12'	**Mechanical Repairs**	no
Accepts Transients	yes	**Ships Store**	yes
Dockside Power	30,50	**Showers**	yes
Dockside Water	yes	**Laundromat**	no
Gasoline	yes	**Restaurant**	yes

Brielle, New Jersey to New York City

The trip from Brielle to New York City is 44 statute miles. The New Jersey ICW ends at the northern end of Barnegat Bay, which is South of the Manasquan Inlet. Therefore, the trip from Brielle to New York City must be in the ocean. Using NOAA charts 12324 and 12327, cruise along the shore to Sandy Hook. Several miles north of Sandy Hook is the Ambrose Channel, which is the main ship channel into New York Harbor. Cruise to buoy G "3" at (N 40° 30.1' -- W 74° 57.5'), which is on the Ambrose Channel. Follow the Ambrose Channel under the Verrazano Bridge into New York Harbor.

The End of an Adventure